Thirty Degrees East

A trek from the Black Sea to the Mediterranean.

T. D. CHATTELL

FULL COLOUR EDITION

Map formatting is provided by
ScribbleMaps™ under commercial license.

All trademarks, logos and brand names are
the property of their respective owners.

For Mum, who taught me to love stories.

For Dad, who took us to Dartmoor.

Contents

Acknowledgments   viii

Notes on style   x

Geographic Overview   xii

Preface: 'Day 0'   xiii

Intro Stage: Kefken – Sakarya   1

Stage 1: Sakarya – Eskişehir   32

Stage 2: Eskişehir – Afyonkarahisar   139

Stage 3: Afyonkarahisar – Eğirdir, Isparta   198

Stage 4: Eğirdir, Isparta – Antalya   255

Conclusion: *"Neden?"*   334

Acknowledgements

As clichéd as it might be to point out, it is nevertheless true that neither this book, nor the journey itself, would have been possible without an enormous degree of help. Although it was a solo journey, it was by far and away, a team effort.

Specifically, in keeping me going through the process of committing my recollections to print, therefore, are a few names I wish to pay specific tribute to. Firstly, anyone who had the misfortune of knowing me as I put this project together, forever rabbiting on about various disconnected tales, can rest assured that now committed to print, I might stop talking about them as much. Particular commendation goes to Ciara MacDonald, Anna Lamport, George Warner, William Rance and Jessica Allington: rest assured, I may stop going on about 'this one time in Turkey' now. Secondly, those who have followed this project from its genesis, and borne with my frustrations and continual missed deadlines, are also worth mentioning. Jack Mitchell, Catherine Saunders, Jack Mason and Ethan Lam have always stood by me, for whom I am immensely grateful. There are more names who encouraged and willed me on along the way, who know who they are.

By way of practical help in proofreading, the following individuals in particular were particularly helpful in the drafting process: Zainub Absar; Ozdemir Baruc; Shayoni Basu; Jessika Dawar; Ella Faures; Kit Fountain; Arielle Indraguna; Lauren O'Toole; Will Klintworth; William Maitland-Round; Love Oko; Thomas Warburton; Kate Rosenstengel; Kirsten Scoggins; Jonathan Sharpe; and Sophie Spencer.

Lastly, and most importantly, this work is a tribute to all those who helped me along the path. Many of their names crop up along the journey, but Lucy Bune, Zeynep Gözen, Emine nur Özcan and Selda Durdu are worth mentioning for going even further above and beyond that which many did.

Whether explicitly named herein or not, it is my hope that this work is a small token of my appreciation to the people of Turkey.

Notes on Style

This text first took the form of a small, black, leather-backed notebook that I purchased prior to setting off. Those scribbled bullet points slowly evolved into full prose for a blog of some sort, the blog became an article, and the article became a series of articles. One dark, rainy Balkan evening, disregarding a lot of sound, sage advice, I committed to turning said articles into a full book.

This text is therefore the compilation of those rough notes, written up under torchlight, over restaurant meals, or sat on rocks on the side of roads. As much as my recollections may vary, the following is the most accurate account of what I can recall.

Just as the challenges of the journey itself changed with the geography, so therefore does the structure of this book. No two chapters are of equal length or equal descriptive depth, and each therefore has something of a different character. The Intro Stage focuses on the initial realities of life on the road, whilst Stage One fleshes such realities out, as I grew in confidence. Stage Two was the most painful, Stage Three the most lonely, and Stage Four was an uphill battle in most respects. Hopefully, something of a narrative between the chapters still holds.

Where doing so adds to the understanding of the narrative, I have provided rough translations to Turkish words in footnotes. As many interactions were conducted in hybrids of Turkish and English, as the language of choice was switched out to whoever felt more proficient, any inaccuracies are therefore a reflection of my poor linguistic abilities, rather than adaptions in recollections. I have left such idiosyncrasies in, as irritating as they might be to those who know the language better than I managed.

I have provided as many photos as possible throughout. However, armed only with an iPhone, a cheap portable tripod, and whichever willing strangers happened to be passing, such photos are naturally of limited quality. Short of re-walking the whole journey with a better camera, there is little I can do about such imperfections. Similarly, it has naturally not been possible to obtain the permission or consent of everyone I have pictures of, not least if they have been named, so some photos of individuals have been omitted. Hopefully, my descriptions of their rich characters have done them sufficient justice.

Geographic Overview

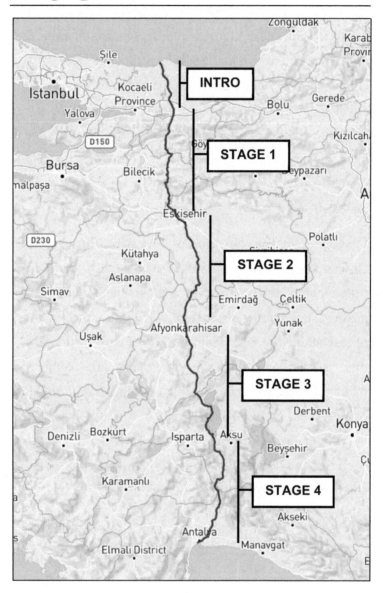

Preface: 'Day 0'

Galata, İstanbul – Kefken Harbour, Kocaeli
30th September 2021

Somewhere between the rolling fields north of Izmit, a yellow taxi wound it's way along, around the gentle slopes and fields, moving downhill towards the coast. The driver had just turned the car's radio off, as the call to prayer sounded across the valleys that afternoon. I think he explained that this was a mark of respect to God, but I was struggling to understand anything he was saying. I was midway through my first real attempt at sustained conversation in Turkish. It was going better than I had mentally braced myself for.

The morning had started early. I had bid farewell to my good friend Lucy and her ever-present entourage of street dogs, which followed her around like a team of bodyguards. I crossed Galata bridge, boarded a ferry across the Bosphorus to Harem, caught a minibus up to another coach station, before getting on a coach bound for Izmit. Once there, I had tried to find another bus to take me the rest of the way to Kefken, but had drawn a blank. At one stage, I flagged down a passing bus to ask where it was headed. As it pulled in, my backpack jerked violently as I tried to re-shoulder it, and I heard a horrible ripping sound.

I tried to understand the bus driver's quick-fire response to my question of 'where to?'. Failing to do so, I let it carry on down the road, without me. I began tying the remaining bits of shoulder strap around the broken buckle, and resolved to find a taxi. Flagging down the first one I could find, the driver was a very friendly individual. As he drove, we conversed in broken, halting language about football teams, our siblings and extended families, and what exactly I was doing headed out to the tiny fishing village, so far out of tourist season. I was already developing a little explanation of the journey I was about to embark on, which only prompted a further *"neden?"* from my driver. Why?

I have struggled to ever formulate an adequate answer. I have few solid recollections of my first trip to Turkey, visiting for the first time in the summer of 2016 to explore the battlefields of Gallipoli on a school trip. Along with some scant memories of gorgeous Çanakkale beaches, imposing former battlefields once assailed by British and Allied troops, and the constant, dizzying July heat, the emphasis placed on Mustafa Kemal Atatürk by memorials on the peninsula struck me. Aside from his memorialisation and subsequent near-mythological status as the founder of the modern Turkish Republic, Atatürk fought at Gallipoli himself. After some scant reading, his wider legacy following the proclamation of the Republic in 1923 briefly intrigued me. After 2016, I would go on to briefly write about contemporary Turkish politics whilst at university, and would occasionally find myself drawn into current affairs there, but never delved much deeper. With a unique position between East and West, Turkey remained somewhere interesting to learn about, and somewhere nice to visit again, one day.

Ironically, it was whilst returning from a trip to Athens, on a short course for students of International Relations from across Europe, that the idea of travelling first seriously appealed as it did. That desire only grew as I moved into London, and found myself surrounded by new people from all walks of life. Residing in an international city, studying amongst a diverse cohort at the London School of Economics, and living with overseas students for the first time, all contributed to a relatively new-found interest in people's stories. Coming from small-village rural Hampshire life, I couldn't have felt further from this new, multilingual world. Able to speak only English, I felt increasingly embarrassed at my lack of ability to master at least one other language, increasingly feeling behind everyone else. This became something of an obsession. *If everyone else could do it, why couldn't I?* The desire to understand more of the world, outside of the confines of home life, became interwoven with a gnawing appetite to, one day, be able to hold a basic conversation in another tongue.

The inspiration for just how exactly I would go about scratching such an itch came from a number of places. Parts may well have been from reading Rory Stewart's account of his own journey across Afghanistan, chronicled in *The Places in Between*. As a Nigerian proverb states, 'You listen with your feet', and I would find myself agreeing with his assertion that walking remains the most intimate, human-scaled way of travelling through a place, allowing the most access to the journey rather than merely achieving a destination. Parts may well have come from a childhood spent watching dramatic survival documentaries. Parts most likely came from my father's annual September expeditions to Dartmoor with my brother and I: around the age of ten or so, we would map-read our way across the moorlands, often wild camping under tarpaulins and repurposed plastic sheeting, huddled around a spirit-burning stove. Wherever the initial desire had come from, a year of Covid lockdowns, shelved plans, and general malaise, steadily made the idea of accomplishing some grand outdoor project all the more appealing.

And so, returning from Athens in the summer of 2020, I began to sound out such an idea with my good friend

Tom. We had met whilst studying at Nottingham, and I knew he had completed a few long-range walks, including in the Middle East. I mentioned the prospect of completing "some sort of massive trek" one day in the future, and he mentioned some daily distances that he had worked with. Not knowing how far I would need to complete per day, I utilised that typically British talent of drawing straight lines on other countries, and crudely judging where Turkey looked thinnest, put two pins into Google Maps. One landed on the first beach I could spot in Antalya. The other landed on a small peninsula on the Black Sea, simply because it looked distinctive. The line that was generated swerved around hills and through cities, meandering across the landscape, but staying within the easting of thirty degrees. Making guesses based on that rough 600-kilometre prediction, I had no idea that, a year or so later, I would be driving slowly north, towards Kefken, ready to start.

An initially academic desire to get to know a country had knitted together two twin motivations. On one hand, a desire for cultural immersion, exploration, and hearing people's stories in their own language would be best served by heading 'off the beaten track', away from the tourist-saturated metropoles. On the other, a deep-seated hunger to do something outside my comfort zone physically, beckoned after the long, lazy lockdowns of the early 2020s. I wanted to do something difficult.

My chances of explaining all this to my taxi driver, after I had struggled to verbalise "anywhere here is fine, thank you", were close to nil. Making do with mime, he understood nevertheless, and left me in the centre of the tiny, quiet village of Kefken.

Checking into a plain, unremarkable cliff-side hostel, deserted aside from myself, was a simple process. With the weight of the pack off my back, I explored the tiny village a little. Kefken looked as though it had started life as a fishing village, before squat concrete houses had grown out from around the historic harbour. They now lined a sweepingly deserted beach of red sand, waiting for their owners or tourists to return with the fairer weather next year. I wandered along the beach, looking out into the Black Sea for the first time, and took a few minutes to swim in the low, calm waves. The water was surprisingly warm for the last day of September, and as I imagined I would get the chance to swim in Antalya, I thought I might as well swim to start the trip, to mark the moment. A stray dog, who had followed me down from the town, sat obediently next to my folded daysack, as if guarding my towel and clothes from something.

Having eaten dinner, and brought food for the next day's breakfast, I updated friends and family to let them know I was safe. I asked Lucy for advice on my already broken pack: my improvised solution to the snapped shoulder strap was workable but deeply uncomfortable, and not something I wanted to rely on. She said she would see what could be done. Whilst updating the social media accounts and re-packing for the day ahead, I listened to a podcast episode from a duo of Australian Youtubers I followed, *Fair Enough*. With nothing else to fill the time, I wrote the Fairbairn brothers a tongue-in-cheek email, jokingly asking for advice on how to smuggle five stray dogs from İstanbul into the UK. I thought nothing more of it.

The next day, Day 1, would be the first on the road. I had broken the trip down geographically, according to where larger cities with hostels, English speakers, and places to resupply fell. I was left with five stages. The first 53 kilometres from the shore, that I had termed the 'Intro Stage', would be the most straightforward. I would follow roads and highways along flat terrain away from the sea, winding up in the first large city of Sakarya in four days. After that, the remaining four stages were all between 120 and 160 kilometres, covering vastly contrasting terrains and regions. The first four days would serve as a 'proof of concept'. It was the place to make mistakes, before the hills started, the mobile signal died off, and I was truly on my own.

I slept with the window open, the low murmur of waves on the shore below a somehow familiar, comforting sound. Somewhere out to sea, hidden amongst the dark low clouds, the next morning loomed.

Intro Stage

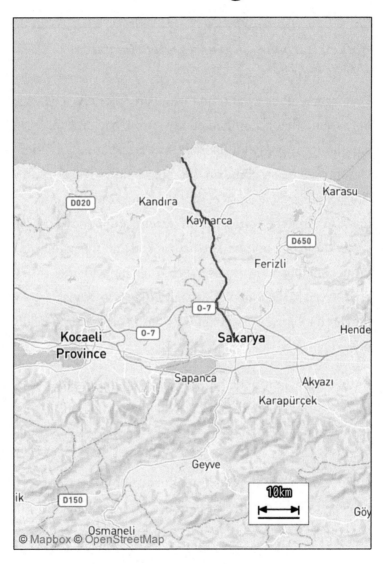

Kefken (Kocaeli) – Sakarya

Day 1: 'When I tread the verge of Jordan'

I can't remember what time I woke up precisely. The only sound that accompanied my frantic packing up, cramming away my kit liberally scattered across the floor, was the waves breaking on the rocks below. The sky sat still, a solid grey mass of cloud, stretching out to the horizon. Breakfast consisted of a *simit*[1] and honey I'd brought the day before. Having packed and repacked unsuccessfully a few times over, struggling with the broken pack, I trooped downstairs. The owner was nowhere to be seen, so I left my dues on a table and made off.

I walked down into the harbour with a full pack, the muggy air feeling thick after the night's gentle rain. Finding a quiet patch on the beach, I stepped over a small chain-link fence and set the pack down on the soft, dark, amber sand. Only then did I realise just how strewn the beach was with plastic, driftwood, and the odd needle. Carefully avoiding such debris, I sat the camera down in the sand, taking a few tries to get the angle right, and

---

[1] A small, baked doughy snack covered in seeds, best enjoyed fresh or with a warm drink.

captured an awkward, nervous photo, marking the start of the journey. Physically 'dipping my toe' in the sea was easy enough, the water still as a millpond within the harbour walls. Feeling the poignancy of the moment, and not entirely sure what to do with it, I sang a brief hymn. I had only just begun to mumble the third line of 'Guide Me O, Thou Great Jehovah', before I was interrupted by a pack of dogs sprinting across the harbour. They bolted after each other, around the grassy verge of the beach, and up into the town, chasing the wind into the country. At 09:15, the morning wet, humid and miserable, I remounted the pack, straddled the low chain-link fence between the beach and the road, and started walking.

It took only ten minutes before I was stopped by old woman asking what I was doing. This was my first such encounter. After explaining I was planning on walking from "*that sea*" behind me, to the Mediterranean, she was amazed, but I was unable to understand much else. As I left the village, I leant into the first incline up from the beach.

The surroundings transitioned quickly. The world changed from beachside village, not out of place on an English coastline, to the empty hulks of seasonal properties, slabs of concrete left until the summer. After 30 minutes or so, I checked my bearings, confirmed the road I was due to be on, and turned a corner. I began down a long, straight road due south, and duly lost sight of the sea for the next two months.

I felt strangely elated. Kefken had felt unreal, as though I was standing on the precipice of a huge leap, not quite believing I was about to launch myself into it. It had felt as though at any moment, someone would point out that what I was about to do wasn't allowed, or that it had all been some sort of extended dream. Yet, no one followed me out of Kefken, or called me back. The morning was eerily silent.

I quickly realised walking in the opposing lane, into incoming traffic, afforded the best warning of oncoming cars. However, dangerous overtakes were surprisingly common, coming worryingly close to the bright reflective strip I had tied across the pack. Passing farmsteads as the coastline receded further from memory, the sun finally emerged an hour or so in. I stopped at petrol station, already lightly sodden in sweat, to adjust the pack. The broken strap was already causing issues, and my improvised strap-tying solution could only fix so much. As I would carry on, the weight would shift to one shoulder over time, pulling me over to one side. I checked a paper map to see how far I'd come, and duly decided that they weren't worth the effort of getting them out of the pack. I packed them back away and checked my Maps app was working. That was the last time I'd use hard-copy maps 'on the road' for the rest of the trip.

As the road began to slope gradually upwards as I made my way inland, the first offer of a lift came by. Driving a van full of scrap metal, he offered me a lift as far as Kaynarca, to which I tried to explain I was headed much further. Confused, he smiled, and carried on. As the road climbed up into the first hill, I passed a child walking parallel to me. He stared, confused, but didn't engage. When he reached his home, he walked into a barrage of furious shouting from a woman somewhere inside. Later on, a man called Mustafa and I walked with each other for some way, him on his way to the mosque for prayers. Sharing the space of the road temporarily, we swapped stories about our dogs at home. Both interactions, only a few hours in, were a reminder of my privileged perspective. Whilst this land was a new novelty for me to explore, for those who lived here, this was their home, and daily existence. I was, I reflected as I crossed my first municipality border into Sakarya, walking through their lives, in a way.

Most of the road into Sakarya sat atop a ridge, giving views out onto the gentle rolling hills either side for miles. Passing Mustafa's mosque, each minaret in the distance began calling out to one another across the valleys. An ambulance passed, the three medics sat adjacent behind the dashboard looking almost concerned for me as they sped onwards. Believing the small town of Kaynarca to be close, I made a plan to try and finish there for the day, hopefully into some actual accommodation for my first night. The two golden minarets of the town's larger mosques glinted in the sun, intimidatingly far away.

The rest of the afternoon was spent dodging lorries and scrambling down the narrow road banks to avoid the passing traffic, surprisingly numerous for the sparse countryside. It was there, on the descent down from the hills towards Kaynarca, that I had my first encounter with the police, who pulled over out of what seemed like curiosity. The driving officer's accent was noticeably crisper and easier to understand than those from these parts. Hearing I was from England, the customary exchange of football team allegiances began. Happy with me to carry on plodding down the road, he and his deputy warned me that residents of Sakarya could be "*cold*", and that I should be very wary of traffic and crime there. This wasn't the first such warning I'd heard about Sakarya, and I took note.

Although by mid-afternoon I was moving downhill, my feet were already beginning to feel done in. I hadn't trained specifically in any way prior to starting, as work and studies had prohibited me from finding the time. I had instead planned to build up slowly during the first leg of the walk. Coming to the end of Day 1, I began to worry that I had overcooked it already. I moved slowly down the hill into Kaynarca, and tried asking the first person I came across about a hostel, hotel, or anything of sort. That first person owned a tiny corner shop, and he insisted I sit down and have some water and as many snacks as I could carry. After hearing where I had come from and what I was after, he rang someone. Not understanding a word of his conversation, I began to worry that I'd caused some great fuss, but he eventually directed me towards a hotel in the centre of town. Just under a kilometre down the road, I felt a great sense of relief to find that it did actually exist.

By pure luck, as I tried to check in for an evening's stay, I happened upon a local tour guide, who helpfully spoke English. Yavus offered to translate as the hotel owner and I struggled to understand each other. Halfway through booking, the phone rang, and the manager answered. After a few questions, he handed the receiver to me. Utterly bemused, I murmured *"efendim?"*. A few sentences were exchanged, talking down the phone being much harder than in person, before I realised I was talking to the shopkeeper from earlier. In his goodness, he had called the hotel to make sure I'd arrived safely. After I'd manage to book a room for the evening, I was asked why I wanted to come to Turkey so much. I responded that it was a unique place, and a fusion of "eastern and western" cultures. This was unfortunately mistranslated as "between Arab and European cultures", and before I could interject, I was informed, at great length, that Arabs and Turks were very different.

Having now found somewhere to spend the first night on the road, I took stock of the small town from a window. Below, the students and staff of a nearby school dutifully recited the national anthem, before departing for the weekend. Recognising the tones was a strangely satisfying moment, as if I was visiting somewhere had only seen in pictures before. Roaming around my floor of the hotel, trying fruitlessly to find somewhere to get some washing done, I managed to completely miss a sign reading *'erkek giremez'*.[2] It was only after I returned to my room, and looked up the exact meaning, that I realised why the look I had got from a woman there had been quite so sharp, my cheery *"merhaba"* left unreturned.

I enjoyed a meal with Yavus and his friend that evening. Wearing sandals to give my feet a break and let the skin

---

[2] 'No men.'

breathe, I could feel the pain of several blisters really beginning to wear already. Walking back to the hotel, I began to, at least internally, panic. *Had I really messed up this early? Had I overdone it, less than 12 hours into what was supposed to take upwards of 2 months?* Fighting these thoughts, I resolved to clean my feet as best I could, and sleep as early as possible. I took one of the four beds in the room, and forced myself to rest. Although only just gone 21:30, I needed it.

I had completed the first day. No one had called me back to Kefken, told me to turn around, or woken me from a oddly realistic dream. Tomorrow's problems could take care of themselves.

Day 2: 'Proof of concept'

Kaynarca Otel, Kaynarca – The roadside,
Küçükhataplı
2nd October 2021

On waking, things weren't quite as bad as I had feared. My feet weren't happy about the day before, but I could still walk on them. I ambled a few hundred metres or so up the road, before happening on a place to get breakfast. I happened across a type of diner, which I later learnt was known as a *lokanta*. A sort of buffet-style restaurant, often serving soups, rice, and various stews all at extremely affordable rates, they would crop up routinely along the way. Two bowls of chicken soup and plenty of bread felt like enough.

Starting the walk out of town, I stopped at a small shop to grab a new, comfier pair of sandals. Before I could do anything about it, I was introduced to the shopkeeper's entire family. Ahmet, a boy around ten years old or so, was ushered inside by his parents to produce his English homework from school, which he duly showed me for approval. I congratulated him on a job well done. Sensing that I was struggling with the language, they offered a phone with Google Translate on, which made the exchange a little easier. On their insistence we exchanged WhatsApp details, and Ahmet, his mother and grandmother bid me farewell, warning me to "*be safe*".

My main worry that morning was what exactly would happen once I left Kaynarca, as I stepped onto a multi-lane highway for the first time. That I would be able to walk alongside major roads, without getting kicked off or run down, was a fairly large assumption that I was now reliant on. Realistically, no other options existed. Turkey is not a country built for pedestrians, especially not those travelling cross-peninsula. There simply aren't any suitable cross-country alternatives available. Additionally, I knew there would be zero chance of avoiding the highway when walking through the Pontic mountains soon. I might as well start getting used to it.

Feeling like I was trespassing, I crossed over to the left-hand lane and began walking along the edge of the hard shoulder, reassured by the flaking white line marking the edge of the outside lane that I was, at least, not in it. The first hundred metres, watching the first few passing vehicles whistle by harmlessly, felt oddly exhilarating. I was, metre by metre, getting away with it. Learning how exactly to walk on highways was something that I got used to. Reading the road from a pedestrian's perspective was a different skill, but one that came easily. Spotting tyre marks or well-worn tarmac around blind corners, where vehicles would stray well over into the hard shoulder, saved a few close calls. Similarly, sticking religiously to the left-hand lane was another safety mechanism. I could spot any approaching traffic prior to it reaching me, rather than relying on the attention of drivers behind me. If a vehicle ahead of me slowed down to stop, I could track it. There was no risk of being crept up on and offered a lift, benignly or otherwise.

Coming off the highway just after midday, mainly to attend to my now-aching feet, I made a stop at the mosque in the tiny village of Müezzinler to patch up my feet and try and find food. The entire village seemed deserted. As I sat on the bench in the shadow of the minaret, a few young teenage boys emerged from inside. Immediately their chatter died down as they spotted me, my unwieldy pack and exposed feet not exactly typical of a worshipper. One lad introduced himself, and in due course his friends followed. Cigarettes were politely offered, and they went on their way. As I got up and made my way back towards the road, an older man waved me over, curious as to what I was up to having emerged from the mosque. Introducing himself as Ahmet, after my brief introduction, he ushered me into his home.

Ahmet and his wife lived on the lower floor of an old shop, as did their immediate neighbours: the forecourts of garages had since been repurposed and were covered in harvested agricultural produce, chickens pecking at the bare concrete. Offering a variety of snacks, he asked what I thought of Turkish cuisine. I replied with the first item that came to mind, totally naïve to what would happen next, that *köfte* were a particular favourite of mine. Within ten minutes his wife had reappeared, carrying with her bread, tomatoes, and a few freshly cooked meatballs, still sizzling from the grill. I was astounded. Via Google Translate on a chunky old computer, I was able to explain a little more about my journey. Pointing to my rough route on a small cartoon map on the wall, he realised I was headed to Antalya, and duly introduced me to his son in the town via a WhatsApp video call. In English, I asked him to thank his parents, extensively, for their hospitality. Keen to get back on the road, we grabbed a photo, and I left them with a postcard of London as a memento of my visit. I had been forewarned about Turkish hospitality, but I was still left slack jawed for the rest of the day.

The rest passed monotonously. On a few occasions, vehicles would spot me making my lone way along the highway, stop, reverse back along their lane, and hold out an upturned palm, as if to ask what I was doing. Over four lanes of occasional traffic, it is quite hard to convey anything, not least in a foreign language. Giving up on trying to explain, I graciously declined any offers of lifts, and was wished well. Overwhelmingly, the day's feeling was one of frustration. I felt limited by my own caution. I was deeply conscious that pushing myself too hard again could put the next two month's plan in jeopardy. My shoulders felt fine. My back was complaining, but quietly. Stamina-wise, I had no issues. It was simply a matter of 'breaking in' my feet: they needed time to adjust and adapt to this strange new daily rhythm. Until then, the feeling of having a speed limit hung over me. Despite the open road sitting open ahead, I would have to wait to get beyond it, into the 'red meat' of the journey.

Nevertheless, summiting a small incline, I reached the village at which I had hoped to arrive. Küçükhataplı lay off to my left, nestled amongst trees along a steep bank. I replayed a brief script that I had memorised, explaining the predicament I had shoved myself into, to whoever might be able to help. I was from England. I was walking from coast to coast, had started in Kefken, and wanted to reach Antalya. I needed somewhere to pitch a tent for one night, and anywhere ("just a piece of land", or something equally clumsy) would do. My initial attempts drew a blank, as the village was simply empty. Eventually, after every house's dog had sounded off that I had arrived, I happened across a couple tending to their front garden.

Explaining my story, their expressions turned from suspicion to warm welcome, and then to awe. I understood well under 50% of their reply, and so the back-and-forth began. I felt discourteous, not knowing how to respond more adequately. After a few halting exchanges, I worked out that there was a football field at the bottom of the village, which I could use. I trotted down the hill from their house, and threw up the tent on a patch of short grass overlooking an artificial pitch, before anyone could stop me. As I plugged the phones into the solar panel, topping them up with the last of the evening's sun, I began tending to my feet again, when there was a patter of feet behind me, and a blur of motion. I recoiled. Instead of an ambush, however, a tiny dog ran up to me, leapt into the air for all of a second, and landed with an affectionate thump on the ground in front of me, expectantly awaiting a belly rub. I duly obliged.

As the evening wore on, a group of kids arrived to play football. Eyeing me nervously, they kept their distance, whilst I made my first notes on the day's events in the diary. Eventually, as with the others earlier in the day, they summed up the courage to come and introduce themselves. Once they had done so, however, there was no respite. I was instantly the star attraction of their group. Sooner or later, their parents came to investigate the fuss, and I repeated the same few lines of introduction

I now knew with building confidence.

As the evening wore on, however, I realised that this business would take a little more getting used to. Cooking for myself that evening – just a simple pasta meal brought from the adjacent petrol station over the highway – went wrong, when I tried to stir in far, far too much powdered tomato soup for the water I had. Eventually, after dark, the group left me to work out what to do with this stodgy mess of my first meal. *If I can't even cook pasta*, I thought, *how well is the rest of this going to go?*

There were very few evenings that I would characterise as deeply unpleasant, but the first evening spent 'on the ground' under my own steam was certainly one. I dreamt, vividly, that the tent was being slowly crushed under some great unseen weight, and my cries of help went unanswered. I woke in a cold sweat, only to watch a shadowy outline creep across the canvas. Eventually I calmed down, and the dog mooching past at 02:00 completed its business and left.

Day 3: 'The universal language of BBQs'

The Roadside, Küçükhataplı – Yusuf's Family Home, Camili
3rd October 2021

I rose in good time, and tried to pack away fast enough that I wouldn't have to explain my presence to many more people. This wasn't to be. Mid-way through breaking camp, I was greeted by the same gang of kids from the day before. Half packed and half sprawled out across the grass, I devised a game with them to play as I packed, embarrassed to be the centre of attention again. I'd hold up each item in turn and say its name in English, they would respond with the Turkish equivalent, and I would pack it away. This helped the process of packing, without ignoring my thoroughly fascinated audience. Before I was able to get going, one of the children's mothers brought out a plastic contained filled with cheese, bread and olives. The generosity on display was remarkable, not only for the food on offer, but the trust that was afforded to me so readily by a complete stranger.

Having finished breakfast, packed away, and re-mounted the pack on my back to set off, the woman who had brought breakfast over emerged from her home again. This time, she brought a girl in tow. She couldn't have been more than fourteen years old, and quite evidently did not want to come and be introduced to me. I couldn't understand a word of the introduction, but the body language of the girl, and her somewhat enthusiastic older relative, gave me a very bad feeling. I exchanged a greeting, thanked them for breakfast again, and scarpered before the situation got any more awkward.

Getting on the road after the first night was far easier than the day before. Having proved the basic concept would work, it felt great to be cracking on. Lunch was at a small rural petrol station, where I stopped to look for something to buy. Before I could, the brother and sister who ran the place had produced a small meal of chicken, pasta, and bread. Despite my protests, I was offered it entirely for free. Leaving after lunch, a car-full of arms waved to me as a group of lads sped away. A few phones were held out, and I felt sure I made it onto at least one Snapchat story. The rest of the highway passed easily, truckers honking their horns to greet my tiny profile silhouetted against the fields.

Breaking off from the highway as early as I could, I ambled through smaller country lanes for a while, passing farmsteads and piles of recently harvested corn. As the lane wound on through the gently sloping valley leading into the city of Sakarya, I passed by a few apartment blocks, in front of which sat two men, watching the world go by. Spotting me, they waved me over.

Yusuf and Faruk were two colleagues from the nearby Toyota plant. Yusuf was a foreman who Faruk worked for. The flat we had congregated outside was home to Faruk, his wife and children. Between Yusuf's English and my Turkish, we were able to cover a whole array of topics, and chatted together as the evening drew in. I was again introduced via WhatsApp to members of their wider family, and after I explained my situation, Yusuf offered me the garden of his father's house to camp in.

It was Yusuf's idea to have a barbecue together. Driving into town, we picked up a variety of sausages, curried chicken, bread and drinks, before driving back up to where I had since made camp, secure within a fence line. The three of us sat around the campfire all evening, talking about our families, our plans for the future, the politics of Britain and Turkey, where we had lived, and how it is that we've both arrived to where we are now. The conversation was halting, but we got by. The warmth of feeling displayed was impossible to misunderstand. Occasionally, we would catch ourselves smiling, half awkwardly and half amusedly, at the circumstances that had lead us to meeting.

As darkness fell over the valley, the orange glow of

tractors and machinery illuminated the fields, as they worked into the night. The light was not harsh enough, however, to obscure the evening's night sky. The hum of distant engines blended with the evening's call to prayer, which echoed across the hilltops from miles away. The night was much colder than I had anticipated, but not impossible. I made a note to upgrade my sleeping bag as soon as I could.

Day 4: 'No Islam, no problem!'

Yusuf's Family Home, Camili – Central park,
Sakarya
4th October 2021

I packed up as quickly as possible. The night before, Faruk had extended an invitation to breakfast to me, prior to his children leaving for school. I wandered down to his, the morning air crisp and cool to walk through. At Faruk's, a delightful spread was laid out: *menemen*[3] (a favourite of mine already), eggs, fresh warm bread, *mıhlama*[4], and plentiful tea awaited us. Faruk and I struggled to talk, but the practice for his English and my Turkish was good for us both. Before we parted ways, I was sure to get a family photo with everyone, and left a few souvenirs of the UK with them for their hospitality. Then, the children got on the school bus, and I got back on the road, for what I hoped would be the last day of the Intro Stage.

It was this morning when the first case of 'Maps got it wrong' occurred. The quiet side-road that I had wandered along all morning was brought to a halting conclusion by a construction site, the path ahead

---

[3] A thick mixture of egg, tomato, peppers and cheese, which is cooked over a stove and often had for breakfast.
[4] An even thicker melted cheese dish, allegedly originating from the Black Sea, eaten with hunks of bread.

vanishing under a wall of thick brown mud. Seeing that there was no way I could climb over or around it, I realised I had to jump back onto the highway once more. I checked that everything on the pack was tied down, waited for a lull in the traffic, and sprinted haphazardly across the four lanes.

Back in my left-side hard shoulder, my next stop was a petrol station. Asking if I could buy some food, I was rebutted by the five workers on their lunch break, and promptly offered a toasted sandwich with cheese and salami-like sausage (*sucuk*). Taking lunch out in their smoking area, I let my feet air whist tucking in, and in conversation with one attendant, heard about his opinions on the tourists that came through Turkey. The Germans weren't commented on, the British were generally racist, and the Russians mostly Islamophobic. I offered my apologies for my own nation, before finishing lunch and wandering back onto the highway, to my new-found friend's utmost confusion.

After a while I was able to re-join my original side-road route, the lack of traffic or distractions letting me sink into a methodical pace that I could sustain for hours. The fields morphed into scattered houses and shacks, which grew into single streets, which in turn grew gently into the outer neighbourhoods of Sakarya. A few hours in, a gentle drizzle began to fall. I walked on, the rain offering relief from the hot work of sustained walking, safe in the knowledge that I had somewhere warm to stay that evening. When the weather did become too much to carry on in, I rested on a bench in the shelter of a newly built mosque. Two older gentlemen asked what I was up to, and I told them the story. They asked if I was a Muslim. I replied in the negative and was told this was no issue. *"No Islam, No Problem!"*. When I mentioned that my dad was a priest, the men were surprised, and almost fascinated, politely. Having been asked about my parents and family background several times by now, I had looked up the literal translation for 'priest'. When that didn't work, I went with 'Imam for a church', which did the job. I would come to occasionally rely on that description for the rest of the trip.

Most of the afternoon passed on the same straight, flat path, running alongside a canal into the heart of Sakarya. I was grateful for the lack of hills. Stopping at a bus stop to rest my feet, a woman waiting next to me asked where I was going. I explained, at which point her bus arrived. Hurried, she pulled out a packed of biscuits from nowhere, threw them to me, wished me good luck, and was off, with the urgency as if I was going to Antalya that same day.

The last bit of walking for the day was into a park in the centre of Sakarya. Relieved to have made my final waypoint of the Intro Stage, I sat down on a low wall, my pack resting on the rugged stonework. Nearby, a father and son served *pide*[5] and drinks from a small kiosk to a group of teenagers who'd just emerged from school. I was invited to have some, and the owner refused any payment again. As I sat down to eat, the group of young people backed off, chatting to themselves in low tones, trying to size up this strange person who'd just arrived. One eventually came and introduced himself to me, at which point his mates enthusiastically followed, asking all manner of questions, which I fielded awkwardly.

Exploring the rest of the park for somewhere else to rest, a group of students, probably just under my own age, waved me over. I got to know the small, diverse crowd quickly, although the fast-paced conversation was much more than I could follow most of the time. It ranged from what I did at university, to where I was going, which areas of Turkey to avoid, and which of the group I most liked the look of. Somehow, a press-up competition was suggested between two of the lads and I. After (narrowly) completing the most in a minute, I gained a few Instagram followers, one Snapchat username, and a cheesy group

_____

[5] A flat bread, covered in beef, peppers and cheese.

photo, before my newfound friend Hasan rang to ask where exactly I was.

Hasan was from a website called CouchSurfing (CS), which works on a simple principle: travellers could connect with local people who offered accommodation, allowing for travelling the world far more easily. Hasan would be the first person I would stay with, and we had agreed prior to meet in the park after he had finished work. Once we had found each other, I noted the exact spot I had reached in the park to return to, before we drove up to his house, fifteen minutes or so from the city. Watching the progress I'd made that day disappear behind us in minutes felt more amusing than anything else.

Hasan made us dinner: *mantı*,[6] with lashings of hot sauce for our main course, and cold *baklava*[7] with cream for dessert. I was offered a room with a roaring log fire for warmth, downstairs from my host. My attempts to ring home stymied by WhatsApp technical issues, I got an early night, breathing more easily than the last few nights.

---

[6] Small dumplings filled with meat and served in a yogurt-like sauce.
[7] A sweet pastry-based dessert, usually made with nuts, honey and syrup.

Day 5: 'OK brother.'

Like myself, Hasan was relatively new to CS. He had yet to host anyone at his place, making it a first time for both of us. He was a young professional, a few years older than I, working at a small export business in Sakarya. He lived alone on the top floor of a house owned by his parents, the bottom floors used for storage and a guest room, where I now stayed. Surrounded by walnut trees in his garden and fields across the road, the sleepy village felt not dissimilar to my own in Hampshire. He was extremely generous, not only in his provision of accommodation and food, and showing me around his village and town, but also in helping me prepare for Stage One, as it loomed. My thin summer sleeping bag, brought for an average temperature that I had got wildly wrong, was traded for a surplus Turkish Army one he had lying around.

Hasan and I had a fairly chilled day, as I aimed to spend as little time on my feet as possible. I got the tent fully dried and aired out, my stinking clothes washed, and everything with a battery recharged. I was shown around Sakarya, met his boss and colleagues, and we grabbed some more food for the next leg of the journey. Hasan's

English was great, so I was able to ask many of the questions I'd accumulated by now. We touched on religion, and I gave a probably too in-depth summary of the history of church schisms. We touched on his plans for a family in the future and his wife to be, a very pretty nurse from Eskişehir. We touched on our families, my Dad's job again generating interest. We touched on what exactly I was trying to achieve in committing myself to a trek of this magnitude. Having an English speaker around was truly a breath of fresh air, even if I struggled to fully answer his last question.

My most significant problem, however, was the question of how to acquire a new pack. For the preceding four days, I had managed to hold the broken pack-strap together with a few well-placed knots. The weight distribution had shifted, making it uncomfortable to carry for extended periods, but I had at least made it into my first rest point. It was in no fit state to go any further, however. Back in İstanbul, my good friend Lucy had been searching in earnest for a replacement, as I walked. Having found one suitable, I was prepared to head back to İstanbul to collect it, imposing a time penalty of a day or so. By coincidence, however, another CS contact of mine was headed to İstanbul, and would return to Sakarya whilst I was passing. Emine, a linguistics student, was one of the individuals who had offered to have me stay in Sakarya. We had texted briefly, and she offered to bring my new pack over from İstanbul to Sakarya, but neither Lucy nor I had ever met her. After some deliberation, Lucy handed over the backpack, a proven brand worth a few hundred pounds, to the complete stranger, trusting that she and I would be able to link up hundreds of kilometres away. We hoped that Emine did not have a particular liking for camping equipment.

I told Hasan about the bag hand-over, and we headed back into town to get the new pack that evening. Having gotten dinner, I managed to completely forget about the plan, and left Emine waiting in some park for an extra ten minutes whilst Hasan and I sped frantically across town to find her. Nevertheless, we did, securing the kit that would keep me on the road for the next several weeks. Unfortunately, Lucy (in her infinite wisdom) had chosen a much smaller bag than I had planned for, making it difficult to cram my 75 litres of kit down into a 65-litre bag. I packed late into the night, my anticipation growing as I shuffled items around, envisaging how best to re-pack on the hills in the weeks to come.

When I had first planned the trip, I got in contact with an American, Matt Krause, who had completed his own walk across Turkey from the Aegean Sea to the Iranian border. He advised me that if you can complete 10% of any project, then you could finish the whole thing. Although only 8.5% of the way, I couldn't help but feel a strange sense of finality. The concept had, for 72 hours at least, worked. I hadn't died. The pent-up adrenaline of over a year's worth of planning, language learning and kit buying, had subsided a little. I had already 'blunted the edge' of the trek. The stories about these people, and their remarkably generous spirit, were so far true.

Although I could already plot my progress on a country-scaled map, I knew that I had yet to be properly tested. A simple fifty kilometres, over entirely flat terrain, following roads populated with kind, helpful people, was never going to be seriously strenuous. I knew that some genuinely emotional moments lay ahead, both imminently in Stage One, and the stages that followed. However, I knew by now that it would be at least possible to reach them. 8.5% was nearly 10%, anyway.

Stage One, the first stage covering 120 – 160 kilometres, would be far more strenuous. Over half of the total elevation gain lay between Sakarya and Eskişehir, and I would be wholly reliant on the remote settlements nestled amongst them. Stage One would be the real deal. I warned off folks at home that my mobile signal might be fleeting soon, and slept restlessly.

1: Setting off, Kefken Harbour.

2: Ahmet and wife, south of Kaynarca.

3: Yusuf (L) and Faruk (R), mid-barbecue.

31

Stage One

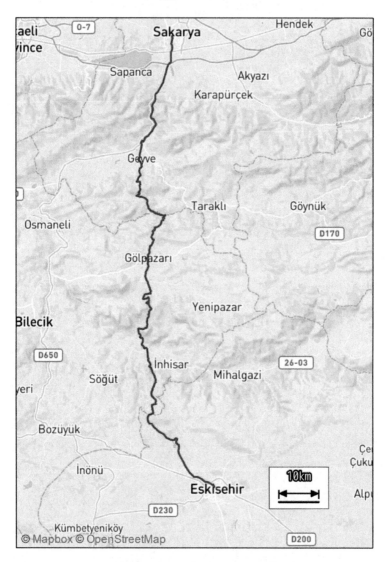

Sakarya – Eskişehir

Day 6: 'Ölene kadar yapacağım' *('I will do it until I die')*

Central Park, Sakarya – Adliye (Emine's Flat, Sakarya)
6th October 2021

Stage One began with a car journey. On the exact spot in the park that I had arrived at, I bid Hasan a cheery farewell. Breakfast was a quick meal of *simit* and honey from a nearby bakery. Seeing my pack, two students asked if I was a tourist passing through, and they explained that they'd come from Thailand to study. Confused as to what exactly I was trying to achieve, the interaction was limited, and I set off along same canal-side track again, out of Sakarya.

The plan for the day was to leave the city via the main highway, and get as far as possible along it. That highway would pass through the Pontic mountains, taking me to the feet of the 'real' hills, and the rest of Stage One. Although straightforward, actually leaving Sakarya turned out to be a surprisingly difficult day. Not wanting to repeat Day 2 again, and punish my feet on the first day of the new leg, I paused to rest more often. Pausing more often meant spending more time on the side of the road in south Sakarya, which was a thoroughly unpleasant experience in every sense. Home to a few huge

33

manufacturing plants, the landscape was lined with mile after mile of garages, vehicle repair shops, petrol stations and idling trucks. The air sat thick with diesel fumes, without a moment's respite all day. The constant exhaust fumes were thick enough to need a mask at times, which I wore occasionally despite the sweltering afternoon temperatures. The hot tarmac below reflected the putrid heat back into my boots, and places to rest were few and far between. I knew that covering the entire country would involve unpleasant stages, and this was very much one. It was not a place built for walking.

As I approached the southern side of the city, feeling distinctly irritated by a morning of unrelenting tarmac, a few voices called out from to my left. I turned, and saw a hand wave from the shaded interior of a fire station. Several figures sat behind the bright red engines, ready to leave at a moment's notice, and beckoned me to come and join them. I wandered over, and was quickly offered *çay* and *tulumba*[8] by the group. Aside from two older men, distinguishable by their uniform insignia as more senior, the firefighters were in their early twenties or younger. The group brimmed with a happy 'ladishness', not dissimilar to a university sports team, that needed no translation. They found my plans very, very amusing,

---

[8] A round, fried pastry snack, filled with honey or syrup.

smiling and sharing boyish glances, probably finding my poor explanation as funny as the concept was ludicrous. I had a few more *tulumba,* before the group insisted on getting a group photo in front of one of their trucks. I felt distinctly child-like, posing in front of a fire engine for a picture, but it would have been rude to refuse. We all found it funny, anyhow.

As the main highway dove south out of the industrial quarter, the hard shoulder vanished over a portion of bridge. After weighing up my options, I didn't feel that trekking into oncoming traffic, around several bends, over a bridge with no space for escape easily, was a good idea. As such, my efforts to try and cross a four-lane intersection somewhat more inventively began. Trying to get a feel of the ground was difficult, only being able to move at a plodding walking pace. I climbed onto the highway embankment where the traffic naturally slowed, where a policeman called over to me, asking what I was doing. He introduced himself in good English as Jihad, immediately reassuring me that he had no relations to religious extremism of any kind. Jihad was not particularly helpful, simply telling me to get a bus down the main highway. My protests about not wanting to use transport didn't land, so I thanked him, and let him return to drinking *çay* with his colleagues.

Feeling far, far too tired to turn back and try another crossing point elsewhere, I committed. Whist Jihad's back was turned, and the four lanes of traffic were stationary, I began weaving my way in a bent-over run through the idling lorries and cars. A few horns sounded. I made it over to the central reservation, hurdling it with very little grace, and paused before sprinting the last few lanes of moving traffic onto the far side. I didn't stop to see if Jihad had noticed. Now encircled by a bypass, I had to cross one single lane bridge to get back on track. I timed how long it took traffic to reach the bridge from the highway, and when an opening presented itself, sprinted the last hundred metre gap. It wasn't a lot of ground to cover, but I was back in 'safety'.

More monotonous kilometres of loud, barren highway welcomed on the other side. Yet, now visible in the evening's sunset, were the mountains I was aiming towards. The highway followed the Sakarya river through an enormous canyon, which had carved the only passage through the mountains in the municipality. A high-speed rail line connected distant İstanbul with the rest of the country through the same gorge, the mountains towering above all that passed through them far below. Seeing them lifted my spirits somewhat, but as I continued to plod on, and the mountains stayed much the same size for hours longer, my morale began to dip again. The challenge had not come from dramatic mountain passes, overgrown paths that had to be fought along, or any natural obstacles so far. Mentally, some of the most difficult segments were of the entire journey were found here, knowing that there was more unforgiving tarmac to go, my feet were playing up again, and I was not yet done for the day. As evening drew in, I set myself a point down the road to reach, and call it a day at. It wasn't as far as I'd hoped to achieve, but it would have to do.

My plan for accommodation was a little different to normal. I had contacted Emine again, and she'd kindly offered to let me stay at hers. I would bus or hitchhike back, stay the night, and bus my way back to the exact same starting point the next day to carry on. I felt that it was bending the 'walking only' rule slightly, but decided it was within the spirit of the endeavour. As long as I was getting a bus *back* to places I'd already walked, and not covering new ground, it wasn't cheating.

I found a spot where locals stood on the side of the highway to catch *dolmuş*[9] taxis, and noted carefully where I was picked up. On boarding, I quickly realised *dolmuş* drivers do not hang around, and I collapsed onto a few unwitting passengers as the journey started.

---

[9] Literally 'stuffed taxi', a minibus-like vehicle that travels along set routes, offering low-cost transport.

Nevertheless, the trip only cost around ten lira (₺)[10] and I had soon arrived back in Sakarya.

Emine owned a cosy little flat close to the park. She had prepared a full meal for me on arrival, straight after her usual work. We chatted late into the evening, covering just about anything. She described her aspirations to become a pilot; how she was now well-versed in many of the original Sherlock Holmes stories after reading them to get to grips with English; how entertaining she found bagpipe music, and if I was familiar with it coming from Britain; and her previous travels around Iran, and future ambitions to study in Ireland one day. We found common ground in our contrasting religious upbringings, having both come from faith-filled homes, yet having learnt to interact with the modern world. After she'd given me a rough guide to a number of traditional Turkish phrases, finding my pronunciation attempts particularly amusing, she asked me about my motivations for undertaking the trek in the first instance.

Common to many people's motivations to travel, I had yearned to understand a different culture, through hearing the perspectives and stories of ordinary people. There was also, I described, the desire to do something challenging. A year of Covid-19 lockdown-induced

---

[10] Around £0.55 in 2021 prices, or $/€0.66

malaise had given me a deep desire to try something that would hurt, and would require a decent dose of serious grit to push through and finish. Coming through such an experience and out the other side held, at least I hoped, an element of redemptive value. Purpose, even if it's just as simple as 'reach that village before sunset', is precious. Emine described a phrase in Turkish to me: "*Ölene kadar yapacağım*", which she described translated to 'I will do it until I die'.

I hoped the journey wouldn't quite get that dramatic, but I appreciated the sentiment.

Day 7: 'A dog called Ozur'

Emine's flat, Adliye – A school garden, Kızılkaya.
7ᵗʰ October 2021

Day 7 was, broadly, a very happy day.

After spoiling me again with a slap-up breakfast, Emine left early to get to work, trustingly leaving me to lock her flat behind me. I caught a bus (or two) back down the highway, roughly guessing the direction each was heading. It took a few, and yet another *dolmuş* trip to eventually end up back on the precise spot of road I needed. Trying to convince the driver to stop and let me off, at what appeared to be a totally arbitrary spot on the highway, made for an interesting exchange.

Having done so, I made some space to prepare for the day ahead. I lay on a concrete wall in the bright morning's sun, trying to wrap my feet in successive layers of zinc oxide tape. I was already burning through my supplies of it, the thick strips congealing into gooey clumps of wool, skin and sweat in my boots. Having ridden a high overnight, seemingly without any real reason, my mood collapsed. *Why was I here? How far down this road would it be before I could go no further, having failed to cross even the 10% mark? Would I ever be able to escape this monotonous concrete purgatory?* Refusing to stay in that place mentally, I had to move physically. I put the boots back on, wincing as I felt the damp inside, and remounted the hard shoulder.

Once again, the constant fumes of lorries forced me into donning a hideous face mask for most stretches of the morning. I grabbed an early lunch of *köfte* at a fairly up-market restaurant, and planned my next moves. I was determined to leave the motorway as soon as possible. The valley was only 200 metres wide at it's mouth, but the floor ebbed and flowed out to around a kilometre wide in places. With a highway and a railway running through it, as well as what looked like small holdings and houses throughout, I reasoned that there had to be other routes as well. The problem was crossing the river, which divided the motorway from the thin strip of arable land on the other bank. Starting off on one side was to be fairly committed, the river being far too wide to attempt to wade. On closer examination of satellite pictures, however, a small footbridge seemed to run parallel to the railway crossing. It offered the fastest route to the other bank, and I was willing to wager that it must lead to the next village along, at least.

Pacing out the last stretch of motorway hard shoulder to the bridge, I found tall crash barriers blocking the route to the bridge. A stretch of barrier had been beaten into something resembling a crossing, and as I approached, a local man got off a bus, clambered over it, and walked out of view into the undergrowth. Assuming this to mean the bridge was passable, I followed him. Timing the climb with the flow of oncoming traffic, which was whizzing past dangerously close, I first hauled the pack over the barrier, letting it drop on the other side, before hurdling the barrier. Pushing through the thick undergrowth on the other side, I arrived at the bridge. Rust peeling in the baking sun, the black paint long having crumbled and piled around the concrete bases, I realised I was looking at the former railway bridge, before the current high-speed line had been built. The central bed of the bridge had fallen away, leaving nothing but the old tracks and sleepers lying across the brown waters below. A thin metal walkway ran along the side of the bridge, made of little more than rusted sheets of steel bolted into place. I crossed apprehensively, choosing my footing carefully to avoid the jagged holes or patches of muddy maroon rust.

Thirty minutes later, I emerged from the undergrowth into the first valley village, Doğançay. Situated on the other side of the live railway lines, I followed another local and picked my way through the fence and across the tracks. The inhabitants weren't particularly in the mood to chat, so I picked up some water and journeyed on. Everything I could see was framed by the mountains, sitting imposingly either side. The continual construction of a new rail line led to a few more incidents of accidental trespass on building sites, but for the most part, the quiet lane wound on, linking single house smallholdings and hamlets. It's quite hard to get lost if you're confined to one dimension.

The day wore on, but it was hard to get bored around such incredible scenery. After a pretty low start to the day, being away from constant traffic and in an area which felt somehow unique was particularly inspiring. As much as I enjoyed the break from urban areas, I was somewhat concerned about where I would end up that evening. There wasn't a lot of unused ground to simply land on, and it was becoming apparent that I wouldn't be able to make it out of the other side in time. I let the concern wait. I was feeling more confident by this stage that, somehow, everything would be alright.

In the mid-afternoon, I settled down to rest my feet, solar charge the devices, and update the journal. With this crude routine established, I felt strangely peaceful, as if I was really getting to grips with this challenge by now. As I rested, a few kids on bikes cycled past, followed by two men and an energetic, buoyant golden retriever. The trio meandered on, offering a gentle nod as I let my feet dry out and recover in the breeze. Planning to stride out the final few hours and seeing how far I could end up in the process, I retied my laces, and resaddled the pack.

As I went to do so, the golden retriever padded back up to me. The two men he was following were nowhere to be seen, and an old, broken chain hung loosely from its collar. It had no identifying tags, yet seemed very happy to see me. Unsure of what to do, I walked on. It followed, merrily. After several hundred metres of his padding alongside me, I began to appreciate this surprise guest more and more. I offered it a few biscuits, and after wolfing them down, there was no getting rid of it. I had a companion.

Taking after Rory Stewart's own adopted dog tale, I resolved to give him a name, now that my first friend was clearly intent on sticking with me. Giving him the first male Turkish name I could think of, after an hour or so of walking, I liked to think he had become somewhat responsive. 'Ozur' was all too happy to pose for a few photos, and as the remainder of the day passed, mostly alone, I was deeply satisfied that I had at least some companionship. I was conscious he was putting in some serious miles following me at pace, and I began to think of how best to make sure he stayed fed and watered in the warm weather. The road had long since become a poorly maintained dirt track, but kept reliably heading south.

As I got closer to the village of Kızılkaya, the logistical problems an animal presented seemed to mount. Being entirely reliant on other people's generosity, I worried that bringing a dog into the equation might entirely change the image that I gave off, making people reluctant to be as helpful. I had barely had a chance to train him, so would be powerless if he began hassling other dogs or people. There was also the issue of feeding and watering another mouth when my own plan for nourishment wasn't exactly secure in the first place. *If he made it all the way to Antalya with me, then what?* I couldn't take him home with me. *Or could I? Would I be able to just leave him? If I was to get rid of him now, how exactly could I do so? How do you get rid of an animal that's attached to you?* Approaching Kızılkaya, I shelved these issues. I would manage somehow.

Kızılkaya was an idyllic little village. Nestled in the floor of the valley, life seemed to pass slowly, as if insulated from the outside world. Chickens roamed freely amongst the small sawmills and piles of timber. Many houses had turned their ground floors into garages, barns, or storage areas, their families sleeping upstairs. A single small shop opened from one such ground floor. Less the occasional rumble of a train speeding by, and the sounds of myriad birds in the trees above, Kızılkaya was perfectly peaceful. Coming to a rest in the grounds of a mosque at the far end of the village, a young lad beckoned me over. I asked him about where I was, and if I might be able to stay somewhere nearby. He agreed that the small grassy patch behind me, adjacent to the mosque, would be fine. I pitched quickly whilst the light lasted, tucking the tent into a corner as close to the mosque as possible, and as far away from the road as I could. Visiting the small shop for some breakfast for the next day, I caught a glimpse of a pack of dogs barrelling through the village towards the river. With them was Ozur, as happy as a dog could possibly be with his new pack, without a care in the world. I left him to it.

As I began thinking about preparing some food for the evening. I was stopped by the mother of the boy from earlier, who emerged from her house carrying a full tray of food. Trying to thank her as best I could, dinner that evening was a chickpea soup with bread, cheese and vegetables. To return the tray, I climbed a flight of outdoor stairs up to the family's main room, in which the senior generations of both sides of the family were seated, enjoying their own food. Feeling extremely embarrassed at my own intrusion, and by my inability to express gratitude in more ways, I briefly described my plans for the next day (promising to leave early) and how I eventually hoped to reach the sea.

Returning to the tent, the sides of the valley stood silent, the night's sky confined to a thin strip running along the river's course. It beckoned ever south, tomorrow.

Day 8: 'Downed pilot syndrome'

A school garden, Kızılkaya – Taşpınar Otel, Geyve
8th October 2021

Getting up started normally enough. Thin white clouds hung onto the sides of the valley, the sun not poking out from over the mountains for hours into the morning. The ground's dew sat for longer than usual, adding another layer of serenity to the scene. I got about halfway through my morning routine of getting up and dressed, getting water from the mosque, getting a coffee and a quick wash from a pan of warm water before packing up most of the inside of the tent. The family opposite me, providing a level of generosity which was now embarrassing, had brought out a few items for breakfast as well: bread, olives, cheese, and a mug of warm milk, the cream sat fresh on the surface. I quietly tried to offer payment or some form of compensation, not wanting to leave these people out of pocket, but it was strongly refused. Just when I thought I'd be able to take in the scenery in peace, several young puppies bounded up from nowhere, yapping noisily as they tried to make off with my food.

And then, a head poked out from the corner of the building. Waving and smiling to conceal my surprise, it did not take me long to realise what exactly had happened. The low building next to the mosque, with the children's play equipment in the front yard, was not as empty on a weekday morning as I had hoped. It was a school. If the two meals provided hadn't been embarrassing enough, a small (but rapidly growing) group of kids were pointing at this stranger who had pitched a tent in their school grounds, and was now enjoying his breakfast surrounded by three puppies.

Their teachers then arrived. With what I can only imagine was a great deal of restraint, they asked politely what exactly I was doing. I explained, and gestured to the family who had lived opposite who (I believed) had given their blessing for me to pitch up here. After some effort to explain what I was doing, shock turned to awe, and the teachers asked to pose for a photo. They explained that they drove in from Sakarya to teach here, and were very forgiving when I offered incessant apologies for possibly disrupting their classes. Some of the children, who I imagined had shown more progress in their English lessons than others, were awkwardly pushed forward by their peers to go and talk to the *real English person*, much to the amusement of their teachers. Turning to talk to the children, the three pups saw their chance. Before I could stop them, all three were snout-deep in the warm milk I was enjoying. We all shared a laugh at the sight.

After a short impromptu English lesson, they headed inside, and I was left to throw the rest of my kit into the pack at full speed. I felt as though I had fallen straight out of the sky and landed in the everyday lives of these people. Before leaving, I apologised again to the teachers for interrupting their mornings, and the classes waved me out in unison. I left the family opposite a postcard from London, thanking them again for their help in the journey. Leaving behind Ozur, the school's staff and students, and those who'd shown me so much trust, I started off again.

The plan for the day was to make it through the valley to the first town on the far side as quickly as possible, and rest in the afternoon before the hills. The town, Geyve, looked large enough on paper to probably have a hostel or something similar. The morning passed quickly, as I strode out the kilometres in the splendid sunshine, and the valley soon widened out. Beyond Geyve, more mountains sat forebodingly, hazy in the midday's heat and fumes.

Having lost the cover of the valley, the temperature soared. My clothes stuck to me, quicky soaking my shoulders and waist where the pack's straps sat. As midday passed, I was getting seriously hungry, and crossed the river into the town of Alifuatpaşa to find sustenance. Walking into town, I had to cross the railway through the main train station. As much as bits of pack were rubbing in awkward places, and my feet were seriously complaining, I ruled to myself that using an elevator broke the 'no transport' rule. I waddled up the stairs, seriously out of breath by the time I'd crossed the tracks.

Arriving in Alifuatpaşa felt noticeably odd. It was a small town, only really put on the map by its train station. Perhaps it was just my own perception, but walking through the centre of town, I felt every pair of eyes affixed on me, without exception. I'd have felt less conspicuous driving a tank. Sitting down to eat my own weight in rice and some sort of meaty broth, a man in his forties, with a black coat despite the heat, and a thin, grey, wispy beard. He asked if I was a Muslim, and I replied that I was a Christian. He explained to me that there were some books that I needed to read, to properly understand Jesus and who he "really was" in Islam. I noted them down. Observing my apparent interest, he seemed satisfied he had completed his job of proselytising. I was oddly grateful this man took the time to try and correct my course in life. Coming from a Christian background, the burning desire to tell the traveller the 'good news' was a feeling of obligation I recognised and knew well. He and I both knew my chances of conversion were slim, but I appreciated his trying, in a strange way.

I arrived in Geyve at around four, as the streets thronged with younger people. Trying to find a hotel, I was directed by multiple strangers over to a place on the far side of the town, and booked into a tiny room for a single night. I climbed the stairs up to the third floor, dropped my pack, and went to admire the view.

I can't adequately describe why, or for that matter what, happened next. Looking out over the mountains that I'd be climbing up into over the next 2 weeks took my breath away. I shed a tear. The hills rolled up from the plateau, covered in a thin carpet of vineyards and orchards, ascending up into great peaks that dominated the horizon. That, tomorrow morning, would be the 'real deal', which I now stood within touching distance of. The 'real' country, lay ahead. No more motorways, petrol stations, or choking fumes, at least for a bit. I was looking at the track less travelled. No one wound up in places like here by accident. Few, if any, would go as tourists. It beckoned.

I spent the 'rest afternoon' doing various chores in town, stocking up on food, and calling home. I acquired a new comfy pair of sandals, which clipped neatly onto the side of the pack for easy access. I enjoyed a kebab in a restaurant run by two brothers: our conversation flowed relatively easily, and I felt, only eight days in, the progress I had made as we chatted away.

Not all such interactions were as successful. I tried to acquire some bread for the next day, asking the family who owned the town's bakery when they were open. They responded with *"seven"*. I asked, *"today or tomorrow?"*, and they repeated themselves, both parties becoming mountingly frustrated at each other. It took a minute or so for the preceding numbers, 'twenty-four', to click in my mind, and for me to understand that they weren't closing anytime soon. We laughed about it, and I laughed at myself.

I spent the evening poring over maps, distances, and elevation estimates for the next few days. Each day now had an 'optimistic' and a 'pessimistic' plan, the distances between clusters of houses mapped out to allow me to adapt on the road. I slept later than I planned to, half out of my late-night planning, half from a growing sense of anticipation for what tomorrow would bring.

Day 9: "Tim, Tim, relax!"

Taşpınar Otel, Geyve – Yusuf's Shed, Alıplar
9th October 2021

Breakfast consisted of rice, chicken soup, and some form of vegetable and beef broth. I ate greedily, knowing that I would need the fuel.

Leaving Geyve, the morning began strongly. I cut a rapid pace through the orchards and small fields that led up to the mountains before, making excellent progress driving through the low trees whilst I was still in the shade. The elevation gain was surprisingly sudden. The first hamlet of the day, Sarıgazi, sat on a steep incline out of the plateau. Trying to obtain lunch proved more difficult than anticipated, and so I powered on up the hill. A group of labourers, working on the construction of a house overlooking Geyve, waved me over, and I shared a few hunks of bread, cheese, and onion with them as a light lunch. A little further on, I paused on an abandoned construction project to re-affix foot tape. Sitting on the unfinished roof, I admired the progress I had made that morning.

By the early afternoon, the path became too steep for vehicles to manage, and I could only do so in short, sharp bursts of energy. As the woodland thickened either side of my route, I became thoroughly drenched in sweat, fighting to just keep plodding up the side of the hill. About halfway up the steep incline, I paused to rest my feet, and let them dry off again.

Sitting back against the pack, looking down back onto now distant Geyve, was absolutely overwhelming. I felt a flash of inspiration, and something like a deeper sense of meaning than I had done in a long, long time. Life had been made simple. Every goal, every objective, was beautifully straightforward. Get to the next checkpoint. Find water. Don't go hungry. Keep going. It was awe-inspiringly powerful to sit back, look beyond Geyve into the valley I'd come out from less than 24 hours prior, and reflect on how far away the sea was now. If I could come this far, and I was now well over the 10% mark, I could manage the rest. That moment, thoroughly intoxicated by emotion, was the first time I seriously contemplated being able to complete what I had set out to do.

I kept struggling up the hill, Geyve slowly vanishing behind me. For the remainder of the day, the path would sink into small valleys, rising again over minor summits, and join and leave minor roads up to lone farms. The vineyards become more numerous as I moved through the hills, deeper into the dense surrounding woods and mountains. As the afternoon moved on, and I got closer to the target village of Alıplar, a couple knelt in a field, presumably to pray, as the slowly setting sun bathed the scene in a gentle orange glow. Through the peace and quiet, rounding a corner came a black Nissan Juke. The lack of mud on the doors and wheel rims suggested that it hadn't come from nearby. The driver slowed down, reversed, and rolled down his window. I mentioned I was going to Alıplar, and he told me to come find him there for tea. A few more turns of the road later, I spotted the Juke parked in the driveway of a house, surrounded by piles of sand and bags of cement.

Yusuf and his father lived in İstanbul. Every weekend, they told me over glasses of *çay*, they would drive out to their construction site here in the mountains, and make progress on building a new house for their family. The exterior was largely finished, and although there was still much work to be done, Yusuf and his father enjoyed the chance to get out of İstanbul to work on it. They yearned for when Yusuf's wife and three children would be able to roam freely though the hills and forests, out of the city. I found their story enthralling, and admired the spirit of tenacity, experimentation, and 'let's see what happens' that they'd brought to bear, scraping out a new home into the rock. We enjoyed yet more *çay,* some bread, honey and *pekmez*[11] under the porch of a shed Yusuf had built, and stayed in whilst working on the house. The shed, composed of cinder blocks and sheet metal, was perched perilously on the side of the hill, but offered an incredible view into the valley below. Sensing my apparent agitation, Yusuf repeatedly reminded me to *"relax, Tim!"*.

As the evening drew in, he offered to let me stay the night with his father and himself. We spent the evening around a fire, with crisps, nuts, and non-alcoholic beers. His father, a devout man, played some traditional Turkish music performed by a relative of his on Youtube, whilst Yusuf disappeared to smoke out of sight of his father. I was, as was becoming customary, introduced to the wider family via a WhatsApp video call. They really had quite the setup. Coming from the UK, where home ownership has become increasingly unachievable for younger generations, I was a little envious that all of this was possible on a forklift engineer's wage. That evening, we slept next to one another, protected from the night's cold under a thick layer of blankets in the shed.

---

[11] A thick, sweet concoction, not dissimilar to molasses or treacle, made from grapes.

Day 10: 'Do you have a gun?'

I washed that morning in the ice-cold water from a hose, perched between wooden pallets, as Yusuf and his father mixed cement. The morning was thick with mist. The view downhill had totally vanished, covered by an impenetrable white sheet that obscured all below. Periodically, a shot would ring out in the woods, and I asked what the source of the noise was. I was told that they were automatic 'bear scarers'. I suddenly found myself unable to remember the difference between black or brown bears, or what to do in case of an encounter with either, or which ones lived in Turkey anyway. Oh well.

After our breakfast, my hosts set to work hauling up the cement through the second-floor window. We exchanged numbers, and I set off up into the hills again. The morning was all hills, and winding tracks through endless pine forests. The journey would be dotted by the occasional logging camp, usually a hut built of timber and plastic sheeting, and (as ever) a few flags. As I got going, the sun burned off the mist, and the air out into the mountains felt fresh and clean. Sadly, as I walked, piles of fly-tipped rubbish became more prevalent. I became irrationally annoyed each time I passed another rotting slurry of plastic, slumped down another hillside. This landscape was so beautiful, and yet so remote. It would take quite a drive to come all the way here to spoil it, but somebody had.

Coming up over a ridge, I dropped down into the village of Çime, a kilometre or so off the route, to try and obtain water. Since Geyve, I was now carrying two litres (one in a nice steel bottle, one in a repurposed clear coke bottle), but made it a rule to replenish as often as possible. Wandering along, a family saw me, and duly waved me over. They refused to let me leave their home until I'd had a full meal of freshly scrambled eggs, tomatoes, and a flat, thin, unleavened homemade bread. The family's cat, pushing his luck with this new stranger, did his best to snatch grapes and scraps of tomato from our table, and was duly chased off. Their children were incredibly curious, asking many questions about the journey and my plans, trying out the English they'd learnt at school. One asked, *"are you ever scared?"*, to which I mentioned the occasional warnings about wild dogs, and it being cold at night. After a bit of miming and improvising, I realised one question that followed was *"do you have a gun?"*. I didn't. The fact that they asked, made me hope I wasn't naïve to not carry one.

After lunch, I expressed my appreciation, and made off eastwards. The day was hot, but progress was mostly downhill, and flanked by cool pine forests and fields. The scene was thoroughly therapeutic, and I sailed down the rolling hills towards the river separating the provinces of Sakarya and Bilecik. At the base of the valley, I came to rest briefly in the tiny village of Sehren. A gentle breeze whipped a layer of heat from me, as my shirt clung onto my chest, sodden. A flock of goats was driven through the village as I watched. One straggler strayed from the flock to grab a bite from a tree, and was beaten back onto the road, the great mass of animal following the route I would follow later. The shepherds stared at me, and walked on.

Crossing the small river, I knew I had left Sakarya province by the immediate change in the style of bus shelter. Although I had seen no buses since leaving Geyve, and wouldn't for another day or so, the shelters were quite common, and marked a strange sense of progress. There could only be eight different bus shelters, signifying eight municipalities, before I was finished in Antalya. Bilecik, where I now found myself, was the third. They were a weirdly encouraging sign, throughout the journey.

The last stretch of the day was particularly tiring, although consisting of a simple stretch along the riverside road up to Köprücek. Arriving in the turn into the village, I was thoroughly done in. A friendly family harvesting apples indicated I might be able to stay in the village, so I plodded on.

Köprücek was tiny. The village was built almost in a corkscrew manner, around a small mosque on a slight hill, with houses backing out into gardens on the river's edge. I asked if there was somewhere I might be able to stay, and a lady shrugged, pointing to the only patch of grass in the village situated at a steep angle under a tree. I pitched before anyone else could say otherwise, far too exhausted to look for anywhere better or move any further. Food that evening was a mix of cheap pasta and powdered soup, again made as thick as workable to replace lost salts from sweating constantly. Staying only a few metres away from the mosque's sheltered washing point, water for heating was easy to access. Despite being within a stone's throw of the tent, the routine barking of a pack of dogs nearby kept me alert, and I didn't leave my walking stick out of arm's length.

Getting sleep in was not at all easy, and I woke up continuously through the night having slid down the hill, curled into a ball at the bottom of the tent. It was a little farcical, but it worked.

Day 11: 'Bos oda var mi?'

The Village, Köprücek –Öğretmen Evi, Gölpazarı
11th October 2021

Having running water in such a close-by, sheltered location, I took the opportunity to have a full wash in the crisp, cold morning. The husband of the woman who had suggested the spot greeted me from his window above, and waved for me to come in. He lived in a small, unevenly built house above the mosque. Set into the hill in the centre of the village, each room seemed to sit at a different level to the next, long blackened wooden beams holding the low roof up. Dressed in a crisp, pressed white shirt, he invited me to join him for breakfast.

He and his wife kept a single room warm, cooking bread and heating water for tea on a stove. I sat on the floor around a low table, and enjoyed *çay*, *pekmez*, chickpea soup and the like, with plentiful bread and honey. In the background, the news played away to itself on a huge flatscreen TV. At one stage I was asked my opinion on something happening, and I had to admit my ignorance. As I departed, he and his wife shooed out a dozen stray kittens who tried their luck sneaking into their home. I was very thankful for their welcome, but was keen to get out of the village, and packed up rapidly. Staying quite literally at the centre of their lives, albeit invited to do so, felt as though I was imposing myself a bit too much.

The day wasn't long as the crow flew, but immediately involved some steep, challenging ascents. I tackled the inclines in stages, knowing by now that my feet needed time to dry out and rest, as often as possible. Although I was soon soaking in sweat early on, rounding each hairpin bend of hot tarmac wondering how many more were left to cover, I was getting slicker at dealing with the fatigue, and avoiding recurrent foot related issues.

Re-climbing all of the elevation I'd casually sauntered down the preceding day, my mind wandered, pondering the motivations which had led me to where I was at that point. As I leant into the hill, an odd motivator jumped to mind, unprompted. President Kennedy, in first laying down his ambition for the United States to reach the moon within eight years at Rice University, famously stated that the project was a choice, "not because it is easy, but because it is hard". For whatever reason, in that moment, the words stuck with me. They had no reason to jump to mind there and then, but blinking the stinging hot sweat from my eyes as I struggled to see whilst trudging ever up, they meant a lot.

My plans were disrupted in the early afternoon. I had planned to hopefully resupply food and water at a village called Taşçıahiler. However, as I could make out upon arrival, Taşçıahiler did not actually exist anymore. Where I thought the village would be, I was greeted by thick, dense undergrowth, piles of bricks, and blocks of timber pointing aimlessly into the sky. There was one modern house on the road, which I wandered up to, and sat the pack down beside. With no car in the driveway, it was safe to assume I was alone. I tried to find a source of water, but no outdoor taps co-operated.

Standing alone in the blazing sun, faced with a steep drop on one side and the dense undergrowth of the old village on the other, I felt extremely exposed. Anyone could be watching me. Although in hindsight my feelings of unease were probably linked to dehydration, I became convinced, once or twice, that something lay out in the undergrowth. In my mind, it was watching and waiting, crouched behind the surviving walls of a home, or peering through the long, brown, dry grass. My very real need for rest, having stormed up to the village to try and find water, was balanced against a very strong desire to get moving, fast.

Nothing came of that uncanny sense. I pressed on, following the road as it wound around the side of the hilltop. The stop that I had planned to finish at for the day, Akçapinar, stood on the top of a small hill. It wouldn't have taken much to reach the top, but in the moment, I became convinced that it would be better to push through to the next checkpoint.

Gölpazari was six kilometres away, and although too small to have a hotel, I found a location advertised as some sort of hostel on Maps. It seemed to have actual reviews, had some form of website, and mentioned rooms, beds, and prices. Tentatively, I rang the number. Having conversations was already awkward enough, but I had never phoned someone in Turkish before, and didn't fancy the idea of talking to someone without body language or other handrails.

Someone picked up. They asked, *"efendim?"*. I asked if they were open, which they confirmed. I explained that my Turkish was poor, that I was walking to Gölpazarı that evening, and asked if they had any free rooms. I didn't understand the response, so restated 'free rooms?', and got a positive sounding answer. It would have to do.

The last stretch out to Gölpazarı crossed numerous fields, the road stretching out tauntingly far onto a hill, behind which sat my chance to rest. A few cars drove by, representing a sure sign I was getting closer to other people for once. They offered lifts, or just looked confused as they sped past. Rationalising that I was nearly there, and a proper meal and a proper bed lay not too far away, I pressed on. Dropping down into the final kilometre or so, I was warmly greeted by every dog in the outskirts of the town. A few town packs eyed me up, but a local man, spotting me and my clear lack of familiarity with wild dogs, threw a few stones at them on my behalf. The pack dispersed, and I waved my thanks. A shepherd nodding to me nonchalantly as he went about his evening, driving his sheep homewards uphill.

Having wandered into town and thinking I had found the right place to stay at, the evening's difficulties of that evening began. Several girls sitting outside the hostel, around my age or just older, said I did indeed have the right place. I went inside, and was given some answer I couldn't understand, but was essentially getting nowhere. The chap behind the desk pointed me down the road into town, towards a hotel, and very kindly the girls outside offered to walk with me. After yet more walking, and the sun rapidly setting, I arrived in the town square to find, shockingly, no such hotel existed. Asking around, I drew a complete blank. I was at a dead end.

Fortunately, a woman I had quizzed took pity on me. I don't know quite what happened next, exactly, but she drove me back to the first hostel, had a five minute chat with the same man at the desk, who then asked for my passport and a few hundred lira for the two nights I planned to stay. I had neither the ability, nor inclination, to question why. I was shown to a large communal room with 4 beds and an ensuite shower, and duly collapsed into one. I never saw the kind woman again. For the next few days, I would have to navigate this very confusing world by myself.

Days 12 – 13: 'On the confusing world of an *Öğretmen Evi'*

As ever, Lucy from İstanbul found what happened next very funny. I explained my conundrum the following morning: I was in something called an *öğretmen evi*, which I understood as 'teacher's house'. I presumed it must be a legacy title, as they seemed set up to accommodate guests. However, the next morning I was somewhat confused to find that all of the other residents seemed to be female, and around the same age as the students I'd spoken to the night before. Lucy became convinced that I'd landed in some sort of female students' dormitory, and refused to let her hilarious hypothesis go. To her credit, it would have explained the startled and somewhat confused looks I got from the cooks at breakfast, and the awkward, harried glances my way from just about everyone else.

My mind was put at ease by a new friend. Sat at a table with the printed maps, I was trying to plan my movements over the next week or so into Eskişehir. As I did so, the manager of the place asked what I was up to, and I tried my best to reply. We got into a somewhat one-sided conversation, and I was recommended a lot of local sights. I only wish I could've understood more of what he was saying, but his welcome made it clear I wasn't breaking any rules by staying. Later that day, he introduced me to an English teacher named Tuğba. She lived in Eskişehir, and would be happy to see me there when I arrived. She explained that no, this place was not a dormitory, but was simply housing teachers and those studying education who were working nearby. I was relieved.

Gölpazarı was a tiny town, sat in a plateau roughly halfway along Stage One between Sakarya and Eskişehir. It followed a central street running west to east, which was frequented by an even mix of old tractors and battered cars. A statue of Atatürk overlooked a small town square. The community was most certainly rural, despite the low multi-storey apartment blocks lining the main street. A few empty boulevards, complete with central reservations, tall streetlights, and wide footpaths, stood silently out in the fields. Expansion had once been expected here, but had never quite arrived.

There were two developments that took me very off-guard whilst I was staying. Firstly, an old friend of mine from London got in touch and explained that she and a friend of hers would be keen to join me for a segment of the walk. Cait was doing a photography course at

university, needed some photos for a project, and
decided that documenting my life and travels for a while
would work well. She asked if she, and her mate Jack,
could come along for a few days. We duly set about trying
to make an impossibly complex plan, co-ordinating their
travels from west London to arrive in a village roughly a
day's walk away, just in time for me to meet them.
Eventually, I committed to staying another night in
Gölpazarı, to allow Cait to catch up with me at another
village, to sync up the rest of the journey. What could
possibly go wrong.

Interest in the trip had piqued elsewhere as well. I had
enjoyed listening to the Australian YouTubers' podcast,
Fair Enough, along the journey. Before setting off, back
in Kefken, I had emailed the show in jest. To my
enormous surprise, the podcast's producer had, a
fortnight later, replied to me. He was keen not only for
the guys to mention my trip on the show, but also was
keen to conduct some sort of interview about the trip
more generally for it. I made arrangements to set up a call
for a few weeks out, when I anticipated arriving in
Eskişehir, and I began thinking through the implications
of such publicity.

And so, I swallowed what remained of my self-respect,
and made a travel Instagram. I can't claim credit for the

inventive handle name, but spent the better part of the afternoon following current friends and contacts and building the profile. I was clearly better at walking than I was at social media, not that I had set myself a particularly high bar in either respect.

I used the rest of the day to get as many other chores done as possible, which mainly consisted of washing clothes and buying food. Wandering around town in the evening to find a more appealing dinner, I had a noticeably easy-flowing conversation with the owners of a kebab shop. It was a moment that stood out. In 2 weeks of landing in-country, I was now able to, albeit briefly, summarise what I was up to. It was a little victory, but a meaningful one. Walking back the same evening, I picked up a small bottle of wine, having not had a drink since arriving. Coming back out onto the street, a large group of men were sat around a restaurant into the evening, whilst another group played backgammon in a café, nursing glasses of *çay* and flagging cigarettes. I realised in that moment, in sight of around 40 or so men, but not a single woman, what sort of society I was now in. I hadn't noticed the same gender dynamic in Sakarya, or for that case Kefken, but was struck for a minute by just how subtle, yet jarring, that demographic landscape was.

Wandering back, I continued to plan out a few alternative routes over some wine and snacks, sat downstairs in a common room type area. Through the evening, a few of the students that I had awkwardly tried (and decisively failed) to say hello to also arrived, presumably to do some work as well. I forget exactly how our interaction began, but one of their first questions was, naturally, *"what age?"*. Once the ice was broken, there was plenty more they wanted to ask. Conversation flowed incoherently from there, dependent on who was speaking and their level of language, which varied in our little group. I can't recall how exactly, but somehow the conversation resulted in me reluctantly being taught to dance with them, in an *"Ottoman way"*, whilst they all laughed heartily. Our hands linked as we danced around the cramped space, one of the girls decided to film our group's efforts on their phone. I have never seen the video, and to this day, would rather avoid doing so.

Day 14: 'I'd rather not have had the story'

Öğretmen Evi, Gölpazarı – Mustafa's house,
Büyükbelen
14th October 2021

I can't remember the owner of the *öğretmen evi*'s exact final words, which he said as he gave yet another firm handshake as I left, but it was something about dogs. Upon reaching the outskirts of Gölpazarı, I quickly came across the first pack. Visible on a wide, empty road a few hundred metres out, I stopped, and planned a new route around. Hiking across the open fields to avoid a few stray animals felt excessive, but I decided it was best not to take chances. Most of the morning was the same flat fields, as I strode out across the plateau, towards more hills on the horizon.

Looking back, the events of the morning felt like lazy foreshadowing. I had crossed the few kilometres of flat ground, and was approaching the foot of the day's first hill, when I spotted the second pack. As per usual, they began howling about my presence, but as they were sat 200 metres away, I wasn't fazed. I'd done this before. I picked up a few small stones, put my headphones in my pocket, and strolled on, a hedge breaking the line of sight between me and the five or so animals.

Thirty seconds later, one after the other, the dogs appeared directly on the track behind me. I reacted as I usually did. I turned round, spread my arms out, and locked eye contact. They stopped, some backing off a little. I turned around and walked on, but they followed closely. With each animal that joined them, the pack became more agitated, more emboldened, and followed me ever so slightly closer. The barking got louder.

I approached a shallow stream, the track I was on fording across. The water ran too deep to keep my boots dry, and I did not fancy the prospects of walking with soaked feet for days, with no means to dry them. Feeling the pack trying their luck, I turned back and made a firm eye contact with the largest dog, stepping forward suddenly to shoo it off, as had worked many a time before. No luck.

Every time I stepped backwards, they closed in, but were now holding the ground they were taking. I had stones to throw, but not wanting to escalate things, didn't throw them. They were too close for that now, so I thought. I began backing off along the stream, to look for another avenue of approach, now walking backwards to keep them at stick's length.

This hadn't happened before. I wasn't scared yet, but was definitely unnerved. There was no clear way this ended. Spotting a shallower patch of stream, I continued to back slowly towards it, hoping that the water would act as something of a barrier to them.

The next moments happened quickly. Keeping the pack to my right, I had edged backwards, keeping them on one side, and at stick's bay, the stream to my rear. From nowhere, a tiny black dog, no larger than the average house pet, bounded up to join in, yapping noisily as it joined the fray. Hearing commotion, I turned suddenly to counter it. Sensing my surprise, the pack pressed in. Panicked, I stepped back, stumbled, and took a few paces back to steady myself. This was red meat to them. The howling became louder, and they fanned out in front of me, now six to one. A smaller creature on the far right, sensing his moment, tried to make a dash around to completely encircle me, but I stepped back into the gap. I had dropped my heavy pack by now and was stood firm. I was motionless, arms held wide, and staff held out, firmly making eye contact.

But none of the usual tactics worked. They edged closer, inch by inch. Every tooth was out, and the larger animals in the centre were visibly tensed to leap. I was completely alone, with nothing but a stick, far from anyone, and more or less surrounded. There was no one to yell for help to. My attempts to de-escalate and go quietly wouldn't cut it.

Something of a fight or flight response kicked in. Sensing that standing still wouldn't stop the larger, emboldened animals from getting far too close for comfort, I felt myself do a subconscious calculation. I reasoned it would be easier to disable one of the smaller ones quickly and reduce the size of the pack at a stroke, before dealing with those who would need more energy. Mind made up, bracing for a fight, I raised my stick over my shoulder like a baseball bat. I lunged at the small dog to the left. I screamed, as much for myself as for it, as loudly as my lungs would carry, "*get back now!*"

The rest happened strangely quickly. The tiny dog scarpered, and as my momentum carried me forward, a second jumped back, alarmed. The larger three in the centre backed up an inch, and adrenaline surging, I bared down at them. They bolted, and with it, the rest of the pack lost their confidence. Utterly senseless, I charged, screaming every obscene phrase that came to mind, before doubling back, slinging the pack on as if it weighed no more than a feather, and bounding across the stream.

It'll be a good story to tell, I tried to reason to myself, striding up the next hill with more energy than usual. *You made it, and now you know how to deal with them for next time.* Yet, my brain's rational side wouldn't work that day. I had walked away, but frankly, would rather not have had the story to tell. I felt sick. Resting in the shade of a tree a few hundred metres up the track, even in the silence afterwards, I was shaking. I swore, not at anyone or anything. The poor farmer who got to chat to me next didn't quite understand why I was so obsessed with dogs. In hindsight, it's likely I mixed up the words for 'angry' and 'fast'.

I trooped on into the next town, collected some water, and was about to move on through when a car wound down its window, and the occupant asked what I was doing. I checked I was walking the right way with him, and mentioned how far I was going. As I walked on, the car pulled away, before stopping. The driver jumped out, called me back, and thrust a loaf of fresh, warm bread into my arms. I ate it a little way up the track with some honey, trying to relax in the sun, slightly more alert than normal.

Most of the early afternoon was spent pressing on through more thick pine woods, on a track which wound round the hills and steep slopes towards Büyükbelen, my intended finishing point for the day. On the final slope before I would meet the village, a few kilometres or so away, my attention was drawn away from the path. A huge rock, a few hundred metres of elevation or so, stood there. The views behind me had been pleasant, but the temptation to scramble up to the top of the hill was overpowering. Fancying a challenge, and because I knew I'd regret not trying to summit this little hill if I didn't, I started to plan. Cutting a few low-hanging branches from a tree, I lodged my pack behind a rock, and disguised it as best I could. I walked backwards from where I'd left it, my back towards this miniature feat of stupidity I'd assigned myself, so as to remember where I'd dumped all of my kit. I took my passport, cash, and both phones. The rest would be out of sight for a while.

Climbing the rock was completely superfluous to making progress. It took energy. It carried a hefty risk of a twisted ankle, or a lost pack. My efforts to just 'nip up the side' turned out to take far more stamina than I'd banked on spending. The scree and shingle slid down each time I clambered further up, and although sticking to the larger boulders provided a sturdier route, it was an exhausting endeavour. The more time I spent on the side of the rock, the more concerned I became for getting on with the trip, or someone discovering the pack. As I got more exhausted, adrenaline picked up to match. Traversing around to miss out some of the looser patches of shingle, I started to half scramble, half run up the side, desperate to get this endeavour finished. Finally, I broke onto a trodden path up to the summit, and paced my way up to the very top.

It was worth every drop of sweat. Looking back over the day's progress, and further past Gölpazarı and all the way to the mountains outside Sakarya, was a liberating sensation. I could look back over the ground covered, and that which now lay over the horizon, with a sense of real, tangible achievement. *I had done that.* I had come from as far as the eye could see, and further, with nothing more than the tattered, dusty pair of brown leather boots I was still wearing. Around me, other peaks and rolling hills seemed to spread out like a grand patchwork, a multitude of fields, vineyards, tracks, quarries and lone houses blending into one another. Behind me to the south, a flock of sheep driven by two dogs and their shepherd fanned out across the next peak. The tiny white flecks flowed across the ridge like a murmuration of starlings. The bells on the flocks were the only sound carried by the wind.

I cantered down the hill, sticking to the winding path I'd eschewed on the way up. I was keen to move on, but fleetingly enjoyed the jog down, and the fresh sensation of moving quickly. My kit was, sure enough, exactly where I'd left it. A few kilometres later, I crossed over a small ridge summit into the village of Büyükbelen. It was a tiny place, of only three main tracks, running parallel around the side of the hillside. Sitting on the side of a hill, there would be no unused flat ground in the village.

Wandering down into the settlement, not knowing at all what to expect, a kind old man pointed me in the direction of a teahouse in the centre, so I tried it. As if to mark the end of the day, yet another dog bounded up to me, snarling, with all teeth bared. I kept it at stick's length, and walked on. I was done with those creatures for now.

Arriving in the centre of the village, I reached the teahouse, obvious as the only place with people sitting around, enjoying the warm evening air. I smiled at the inquisitive faces, introduced myself, and our conversations flowed from there. The teahouse was owned by a kind elderly gentlemen called Mustafa, who stood at just less than my 5'4 height. He wore thick lensed glasses, covered in a slight film of dust, behind which he squinted hard at me. Despite his age and slight frailty, he was very animated when he spoke, moved, or did just about anything. He was enthused by my story so far, and when hearing that I was after some place to pitch a tent for the night, one-upped me considerably.

He led the way to a house that I'd passed on the way in, brought out some blankets and bedding, and let me have one of the furnished rooms on the first floor entirely to myself. He explained that he had family who had moved away, and that he lived above the teahouse, so I would have the house to myself. I was in awe at his instantaneous goodwill, generosity, and trust. The ground floor of the house had no walls, but was a storage space for wood, equipment, and probably animals, I sensed. Upstairs had running water from a single sink in the hallway, and even I had to duck through some doorframes. The room I was in overlooked the village through a small, cobweb-covered window. I had a few power sockets, a bed to myself, an indoor toilet of sorts, and a stove. Luxury.

After I'd dumped my pack, he led me back to his teahouse for a meal of soup, bread, *pekmez*, and the like. Mustafa was very invested in seeing me enjoy each aspect, and it took considerable persuading once I was full that I didn't need any more. Adorning each wall were pictures of Atatürk, flags adorned with his face draped over most spare patches of masonry. I asked Mustafa if he was named after Atatürk, and his face lit up that I recognised his hero. As the evening passed, more of his friends joined us, and I was introduced to most of the village one by one. One asked if I had an opinion of *"Turkey's policy in Libya and Syria"*. I replied that I didn't. Motioning that I needed to rest after the day that I'd had, we all walked back along the 200 metres of track that was Büyükbelen. The night's call to prayer sounding from the tiny mosque the village was built around. It sounded intimate, somehow.

That evening, I managed to find scraps of mobile signal by holding my phone in the right part of the room. I was catching up with my favourite Australian podcast, when they mentioned an email from a guy called Tim. Grinning ear to ear, I let the episode run on, and began wondering what I might wind up saying on air, one day.

Day 15: 'That's not fun.'

Mustafa's house, Büyükbelen – An orchard by the river, Yakacık
15th October 2021

As was my ritual at this stage, the morning started with instant coffee out of a green plastic mug, from water I'd heated on my stove. Once I'd packed up and left, I swung by Mustafa's teahouse, and left another postcard of London, writing a quick message to thank him for his generosity. We grabbed a photo together. As I was leaving, a tall man asked if he might be able to take a photo of my passport. Panicking, as I'd never been asked this before, and couldn't understand why he'd need it for any reason other than identity theft, I claimed it was at the very bottom of the pack. The tall man shrugged, and I departed Büyükbelen without issue.

Having arrived as dusk was rolling in, seeing Büyükbelen as the sun rose was truly beautiful. It was an idyllic little place. I stopped as I took the track out of town, just to get a few more photos of that small cluster of houses, perched along no more than three tracks. The rest of the day passed with more or less no human contact. My original route plan shifted slightly. Having studied the route on satellite photos, it seemed as though there was a shorter path available, unmarked on Maps but clearly visible from the air. Risking it, I was able to cut off a few kilometres, and spent the day on a largely pleasant, if uneventful, hike through thick forests and across spectacularly beautiful ridges. The landscape was dotted with quarries, the occasional streaks of bright white rock standing out like scars cut into the landscape. Most of the route was downhill or along contour lines, which made for relatively plain sailing. Whenever I'd stop to rest my feet, I would also ensure that I got a solar charge on for my headphones, two phones, and battery pack. It was best to use the sun whilst I still had it.

On the last approach to the village of Yakacık, the path became steeper, and my hatred of walking downhill was renewed. Yakacık was my target for the evening, but Akçasu was the name of the tiny settlement closer to me on the north bank of the river Sakarya, which had meandered back round onto my path again. Akçasu would have been lovely, were it not for the decaying piles of rubbish dumped on the approach, and strewn throughout the village. It seemed to be something of a pattern: whenever the landscape, whether built or natural, got too nice, someone would spoil it somehow.

I arrived at the bridge leading into Yakacık that Cait and I had agreed to meet at in good time, but spent longer than usual finding a place to pitch a tent on. My original plan was under the bridge itself, which seemed sheltered from the elements and relatively clean. After deliberation, however, I wagered that if anyone (or anything) else wanted shelter that evening, it would come here, which was a potential confrontation I didn't need. I moved the tent out into the woods along the riverbank, sure to place myself under as much cover as possible. If you might be unable to get permission, don't ask for it.

I spent far too long on this, however. It was time that should have gone into finding some form of food, or preparing something with water I should have collected. By the time I was finished pitching, darkness was falling, quickly. Having pitched a little distance from the road, I took note of where exactly I was on the What3Words (W3W) app. I wandered across the bridge into Yakacık, coming back into mobile signal as I did so, and picked up a message from Cait. Her and Jack would not be able to get to me that evening, so we would meet instead at the next village the following day.

Yakacık had a tearoom, at which the locals were enjoying their evening in. I tried to ask if I might buy some food from them, but they said that they could only serve tea. I was given a rundown of the local attractions, however, and learnt a lot about Söğüt nearby. Someone offered me a lift, several times, but I declined. I was seriously hungry by this point. A stroke of luck was the only reason I ate that evening. The owner of the teahouse said something about some form of delivery coming soon, which I couldn't understand. However, sure enough, a van filled with refrigerators in the back pitched up, and the teashop owner motioned for me to follow. I was offered cheese and doner meat, packaged ready for retail, and brought as much as I envisioned being able to carry and consume within a day or so. I thanked all involved profusely, but I don't think any of them stopped being confused by the interaction.

Walking back through the village, I approached the bridge. Just shy of it, I froze. Three dogs had trotted out from the path on the right, and had seen me. They froze. None of us knew quite what to do. I immediately tensed up. A repeat of south Gölpazarı, but in the dark, was not a fun prospect. In that moment, a woman leant out of a window, and hissed at the dogs. They turned, and slunk into the darkness. I thanked her profusely, and marched into the night.

I crossed as fast as I could. Turning back, the pack were now sat on the other side, their shadows cast large onto the road by a lone streetlight. They watched as I dived into the trees on the river's edge, and struggled through the darkness back to my tent, feeling my way along the contours and roots. I ate in absolute silence, alert to even the crack of a branch breaking a field away. As I sat there, alone and vulnerable, straining my ears to the sounds of the night did nothing to calm my nerves. I hadn't felt as exposed since starting the trip. Raw fear sat in the pit of my stomach. In worrying so much about disgruntled humans finding me, I had removed any hope of help coming, should anything else bother me during the night. I slept lightly.

Day 16: 'Two's company, three's a crowd'.

An orchard by the river, Yakacık – A hilltop, Hisarcık
16th October 2021

The world felt a lot more manageable the next morning. The nearest mosque being situated over the river, I packed what I needed for breakfast into a small rucksack before heading back over. I had stocked up on a variety of pasta I'd only ever seen in Turkey, which looks at first like broken spaghetti: being smaller, it cooked much faster, and I could carry more. That morning's 'mosque pasta', with white cheese and strips of lamb doner meat, was particularly satisfying. Another day, another small victory.

Breakfast was cut short by the arrival of rain. As soon as the first shower passed, I ran as fast as my sandals would let me back to the tent, to try and get it down before the next downpour. I got about halfway, but there was no avoiding a light shower midway through breaking camp. Knowing the rain could have been heavier, and that I would soon warm up as the day's walk started, I re-saddled the pack, and crossed that horrid bridge for the last time.

As the day before had finished up in a river valley, a fairly constant uphill trudge to Samri awaited. The track snaked up the slopes, each hairpin bend representing another leg up the hill. The morning's showers gone, it was exhaustingly hot, exposed work, and I stopped more than would usually for water. A lone shepherd drove his goats along a stretch with me for a bit, before disappearing into the undergrowth again. The only vehicle was a single taxi, which overtook me close to the top of the hill. I had a sneaking suspicion that I knew who it was carrying. Sure enough, on the main route into the village of Samri, two figures stood waiting for me as I rounded the last bend in the road.

Cait and Jack had already had quite the experience getting here from İstanbul, but I was just grateful we'd actually found each other. We rested our bags on benches in Samri, and began our length of journey together with a few cups of çay. The local men were extremely interested in all of us, and for the first time in my life, I found playing the role of an interpreter. This was a new experience. My translation was likely all wrong, but we got our cups of çay, and everyone seemed content. I couldn't have been more satisfied.

Before we moved off, I picked up some proper food from a shop, which only seemed to be open if you asked the right man to open it for you. Stocked up on tinned tuna, bread, more biscuits (which I was getting through at pace) and as much Haribo as could be carried, our little trio parked ourselves on a verge, overlooking our route up into the next valley. Cait had already begun to take photos of everything around her, whilst Jack did most of the kit carrying. I pondered just how wise it had been to bring along fellow travellers, even for just two days, and tried to work out how the awkward dynamics of inter-village walking would change when one became three. It was far too late to do anything now, though. We'd muddle through.

The rest of the afternoon's journey followed the course of a steep valley. The first kilometre or so was a mess of construction lorries, passing spaces on the road dug out of the sides of the rock, and dust fumes sitting thick in the air. Our progress was halting, to avoid being hit by anything. When we got to the construction site, our path vanished. Somewhere between us and the track on the other side of the valley had been the crossing point. Since then, the lower foundations of a huge dam had been built, the lorries dumping tonnes of earth into the base of the site for rollers to compact down. I try the nearest construction worker for advice. He said very little, but his friend threw himself into welcoming us with a disarming enthusiasm. He told us, merrily, to just carry on and walk through the chaos, before handing me a pickle he was about to eat and giving me a hearty slap on the back. It would have to do.

Reaching the track required climbing over the façade of the dam that had been built so far, and across a few tributary streams, but we finally got back onto a recognisable road. The rest of the day was an ascent up into the valley. Although the incline remaining mercifully gentle, by the end of the day, I was the most fatigued of our little team. Stopping to chat to a local woman, I explained our story, and asked if she could recommend anywhere we could camp. Her expression warmed from confusion to welcome as I explained how far I'd come so far, and after offering us some bread and tomatoes, she recommended the top of the next hill.

We made camp on the only patch of flat ground we could find, just off the very top of the hill. Facing due north, we had a superb vantage point of the village of Hisarcık, and the whole valley we had spent the day ascending. Before darkness fell, we had a visitor. The owner of a farm west of our camp, several hundred metres away, had wandered over, not to move us on or ask us to leave, but to offer us (another) bunch of fresh tomatoes, and check if we needed anything else. We accepted them thankfully, and we watched as he returned to his small hut, stood by itself in the fields.

For the first time, and on Cait's insistence, we made an actual campfire, rather than relying on my gas stove. Only coming for two days, they'd fortunately brought some dried camping food, which we mixed in with the tomatoes to go further. Stewing over the embers of our campfire, we sat in silence as that evening's call to prayer echoed up from Samri, Hisarcık, and the myriad other tiny villages dotted through the hills. It was a supremely peaceful moment. Now with company, I felt comfortable lying out for a little longer, watching the night's sky slowly unfold, the stars unpolluted.

Day 17: Backgammon champions

A hilltop, Hisarcık – A man's house, Uludere
17th October 2021

I insisted the night before that we leave at 0930, not wanting my new teammates to hold back my progress. As it happened, I was the only one scrambling to get the tent down in time at 0925, whilst they enjoyed a peaceful mug of hot chocolate, perched on a boulder, looking back over the valley. Our view was obscured again by thick, puffy, white clouds, which adorned the distant hilltops that we had passed the day before.

Fortunately, the next few days would be fairly simple by way of navigation, as it was simply a matter of following the country lane to Eskişehir. Unfortunately, at the altitude we were at, we were engulfed by thick mist within half an hour of starting uphill once more. Soon everything exposed was sodden wet, and everything over 200 metres away was invisible. It was tolerable weather to plod up the gentle incline for hour after hour in, but got cold quickly when we'd stop to rest.

Reaching our midway point for the day, another tiny farming village called Ortaca, we stopped in a bus shelter to have some lunch. Ortaca was near silent, save for the occasional tractor and the lulling of cattle. The road's surface blended into the village as it arrived, transitioning from muddy ochre to the dark brown of cow dung and thick, congealed mud. I was halfway through some bread and tinned tuna, having donned a fleece to stop shivering quite so much, when an old lady hobbled out of the mist and fog.

She wore a grey, faded hijab, a thin, dark blue cardigan, and a long, purple skirt, which dragged slightly in the mud. Pushing an empty wheelbarrow, she was very difficult to actually understand. I tried, but felt it almost impossible to get through to her. She motioned for me to follow, and so I did. She continued round to a pile of damp logs, which had been left exposed to the elements, and began loading them into the wheelbarrow. Having offered help, and got no response, I simply cracked on instead, piling the logs into the wheelbarrow. She seemed thankful. I picked up the wheelbarrow, she began moving back in the direction she'd come from, and I followed. I handed the wheelbarrow over to Cait when we passed the bus shelter, so I could hurriedly throw my fleece layers away.

Jack and I followed Cait and the woman down a muddy street, into the thick, impenetrable mist. The village was still deathly quiet. Understanding that she wanted the logs inside her house to dry out, we all set about getting them in for her, leaving the logs around a fire. She didn't seem particularly pleased, thankful, instructing or anything, but simply let us follow her and take some of the load on ourselves. Once we were done, she motioned for us to sit inside, and she began bringing through some tea, biscuits, and bread. I expressed how thankful we all were, and that Cait and Jack couldn't speak Turkish, but nothing I said seemed to register. We talk about our families, as I often have done by this stage of the trip, and she explains how her children and grandchildren aren't around, or had left for somewhere, or weren't here. As she expanded, I was only able to understand fleeting words. It became clear that she was really quite distressed about her family moving out, and as she became more emotional, I understood less, and had less idea of what to do. I tried to console her, but it didn't work, loud sobs now breaking up the thick sentences. I decided that the most respectful thing I could do was simply to listen. I wasn't able to understand, but giving her my undivided attention was the next best, most dignifying thing I could think to do.

Time seemed to crawl past. Unexpectedly, her sister and grandson arrived, and having worked out who the three strange foreigners in their grandmother's house were, reassured us that things were fine. I had a halting conversation with her grandson, who was studying medicine in Eskişehir, excitedly explaining to him that that's where I was headed.

The entire encounter was immensely uncomfortable. Not being able to do anything more than nod, as our host was clearly pouring out her life story to three strangers, made me badly yearn for a much better understanding of the language than the one that I had. If I couldn't understand and console, the next best thing I could offer was at least some attention, and a wheelbarrow or two of sodden logs.

Leaving Ortaca was yet more winding, muddy tracks. Dense fog obscured everything. Having only the bends in the road and the odd bridge over a ditch to navigate by, the forests stopped abruptly. Barren moorland took over, which allowed me to pinpoint just where we were. The ground was marked by no signs, and our arrival by no fanfare, but we had just left Bilecik region. We were now in, at least the region, of Eskişehir. I was far more excited by this than the others.

The lane wound downhill from there, and the clouds we had been walking in all day melted away. Miles of moorland rolled on: a flock of white sheep in the distance was the only interruption of the coyote-brown scrub. A few more kilometres of uneventful terrain, and we pitched up in Uludere, our target for that evening. Five minutes after arriving in the village, a man yelled at us to stop. He charged out of his house, minding his step to avoid the piles of cattle dung in the road, and handed me a fresh loaf of bread. It was hot to the touch, and we had to let it cool for a few minutes before tucking in. As quickly as he arrived, he disappeared back inside, a child waving at us from the doorway as we wandered into the village centre.

Uludere was a thriving place. Resting our packs and enjoying our bread on some benches for a minute, we were all invited into the teahouse almost immediately. Inside, the air hung thick with cigarette smoke and happy chatter. I explained to the group who had invited us in what we had been up to, and a small crowd gathered, eager to listen to every detail. Jack, meanwhile, had spotted a backgammon board. He had been keen to play since arriving in country, and word got round. An older gentleman, apparently one of the better players in the village, challenged him. Although the Turkish side won the inaugural international backgammon championships, apparently it was a *"close"* result. I had no idea if it was or not, but it certainly seemed well contested by the numbers who spectated.

Whilst everyone was relaxing, I found it impossible to join them and switch off. I was just keen to find somewhere to stay, to get watered and fed, and get to bed. Having mentioned this to our new-found pals, I was told to *"hang on"*. A few phone calls later, and someone assured me that one of the men would be happy to host us for the evening. I had very little idea as to where, who or why, but rolled with it. I tried to re-join the backgammon crowd, but still found it hard to concentrate.

We were ushered into a car, and five minutes along the route already travelled, we were shown into one of the men's houses for the evening. He was one of the quieter, older characters from around our backgammon table, and didn't give much away about his livelihood, friends or family. We were assigned guest rooms, and I made it a priority to have a shower, and later helped our host with making dinner for the evening. I was delighted to see that we were having *menemen*, along with a full spread of bread and soup for starters, finished off with honeycomb and *çay*. We retired that evening with a few beers, nuts and crisps to the living room, and were introduced to the rest of our host's family in Ankara via video call.

We had made good progress that day. My new teammates had kept up with the pace with no issues whatsoever. My plan for the next day was ambitious. Cait and Jack would head to Eskişehir by bus and fly home, having got what they needed. I was going to attempt to make it all the way in, in one day, to finish off Stage One entirely.

Doing so would be the furthest I'd walked in a day thus far, at twenty five kilometres. I would need an early start.

Day 18: 'A dog called Alara'

A man's house, Uludere – Deeps Hostel, Eskişehir
18th October 2021

Just as before, my inability to pack at pace held everyone up. After breakfast, and a farewell to our generous host, we walked back into the centre of the village. Here, the team parted ways. Cait and Jack wished me the best for the rest of the journey, and I crossed the muddy village square, and strode out into the fields. This would be the final push of Stage One.

Eskişehir had developed a near-mythical status in my mind by this stage. The little reading I'd done about the area indicated it would be quite a pleasant place to arrive at, and I longed to do a bit of tourist-ing after a lot of walking. Getting there would not just represent having covered nearly one third of the total distance. It would be the first 'real' stage of the journey finished. Leg 1 included around half of the total elevation gain, and represented the first full transition from built-up, to fully rural, and back to urban. If I could pitch up in Eskişehir, nothing afterwards would be impossible.

Most of the morning was a quiet lane, running through the last few hills before the landscape completely flattened out. At that stage, without distractions, little pains and discomforts became more noticeable. Miniscule points where the pack would bite into my side, or the waistband would press my belt into rubbed-raw skin, felt larger. There was little mental escape when the only landscape for miles was the same barren, rolling, coyote-brown scrubland. Images of Dartmoor came to mind, and not positively. Having now left the protection of a shallow valley, the temperature dropped off noticeably.

There was one village between where I was and the furthest outskirts of the city, Eğriöz. Arriving there felt distinctly different to the other villages I'd passed through. I can only imagine that being within driving distance of Eskişehir incentivised car ownership, and thereafter commuting, because the village felt absolutely desolate. There was no communal life to be found, but instead every home stood isolated, separated from the outside world by high fences, automatic gates, and large driveways for presumably large cars. Off to my left, sat above me on a verge, I spotted a handful of wild dogs, and prepared myself for the encounter. I knew by now that the 'suburban' outskirts of major cities were the worst areas for dogs: the outskirts provided a liminal space between 'wild' and 'stray', with few people to control them, and plenty of food. The pack soon lost interest, but one dog from the other side of the road kept following me. It was acting unusually, remaining completely mute, but most definitely alert, ears up and eyes fixed on me. It followed at a distance, staying unnervingly quiet as it did so. My feet complaining from the morning's going, I dropped the pack at the foot of a telegraph pole, and slumped onto the side of the road. The dog crept closer. It dropped into a ditch next to the road, and wriggled forward on its belly, as if to avoid my reach as it squirmed past around me. I sat still, and held out a hand. Only then did it crawl forward into arms range, nervously, before throwing itself onto its side and rolling victoriously in the roadside's dust, tail wagging, eyes alive with excitement.

'Alara', despite being a reasonably large German shepherd-esque breed, was very timid. She took long enough to introduce herself, but once she had done, remained steadfastly beside me. She would occasionally get into staring contests or skirmishes with local dogs as we left the village, but I knew there was little to be done by this point. She would rarely start the fights, and where confrontation found her, she would shrink from it. I didn't have much food past biscuits to offer her, and it was a long way to Eskişehir, I was at a loss as to how the encounter would end. As the seemingly endless road wound onwards into scrubland again, before dipping into the far suburbs of the city, I grew frustrated with her. She was only going to wear herself out following me, and probably had better chances out here where she could swerve fights and scavenge freely. At one point, she

102

drifted off to sleep as I rested on the side of a road, and I tried to pack up quietly and escape. It didn't work, and she doggedly trotted along beside me. I was again, as much as I moaned at her for being stupid enough to join me, grateful for the company.

The road pushed over a ridgeline, and my view opened out. It was still a good 17 kilometres out to Eskişehir, representing the majority of the day's effort. But, glinting in the sunlight, the low profiles of multi-storey glass buildings were now visible.

The very outer suburbs of the city were, just as Sakarya and Gölpazarı had been, not pleasant. As Alara and I made our way down a sloping road, a few hundred metres from the main road into the city, a group of three dogs appeared ahead. They were all smaller than her, but much more energetic. At first worried for my own safety, I picked up a few rocks and carried on, locking eye contact. This time, though, they weren't interested in me. Despite my late attempt to intervene and scare off the trio, they dived towards us, and Alara bolted at full pelt up the hill we had just walked. Despite her speed, they were gaining on her up the hill. And then, she took a right turn, they followed, and I never saw any of them again. Although now free of a logistical burden, I couldn't help myself but feel extremely angry. I had been deprived of a second dog. Although stupid, she had displayed a fairly defined character for the few hours she'd accompanied me. We hadn't even finished the day's walk, and I'd have to do the rest alone. I was irrationally livid. The next few strays on the side of the road earned themselves some stones, and I took more glee than usual watching them run off into the litter-strewn undergrowth.

Lunch was a late one, but I was able to find the first real restaurant on the journey in. It was contained within what in summer would've been a small petting zoo, but on an overcast October afternoon, it was deserted but for a few families. I had a very large meal and chatted with one of the staff members who'd moved from Afghanistan. She expressed relief that I was an English speaker and told me that since fleeing that year (before the chaotic summer of 2021) she had seriously struggled to learn Turkish. English was her second language, behind Pashtun, and she was glad for the rare chance to use it. Having explained why I'd appeared out of nowhere, huge baggage in tow, all the staff bid me a warm farewell as I started again on the long, straight road into Eskişehir.

Day 18 mostly consisted of this one straight road. On it, I watched the transition of fields into extended village, into suburb, into outer city, into metropolis, roll along in real time. More people meant more open shops, and more transport. Houses got smaller, but became more alive with the passing distance. The road itself grew, seemingly organically, into a busier, wider highway, eventually becoming difficult to cross over. I had to dash over once or twice, when the pavement vanished under seemingly omnipresent construction works. I stopped a few times to rest my feet, attracting more attention each time I did so with more and more bystanders present. I found becoming more and more self-conscious. More and more people my own age, a rarity in the countryside, stared at the ragged, largely mute foreigner who marched past.

Getting closer to the city, my route deviated from the highway, onto a quieter road through what was recognisably urban. As gentle as the transition from urban to rural had been thus far, in a moment, I was in what was undoubtedly a city. Rounding a corner, all of a sudden young people thronged the streets. A tram nosed its way through thick traffic, running along a boulevard centred around bright green foliage. Children ran around the feet of young parents, whilst bicycles and electric scooters meandered through the crowds of pedestrians. There was still some way to go. As much as I was energised by the prospects of nearing my goal, the last few kilometres as the evening wore in that were the hardest.

The last break I gave myself was on a small, grassy verge, outside the University. Leaning the pack against my stick, I lay down in the close-cut grass, and breathe slowly. I ignored the sounds of voices walking next to me, which hushed themselves as they came closer. The sun was slowly setting, but this time, I was surrounded by the constant, vibrant music of activity. I gave myself ten minutes, before re-saddling. By the time I was nearing my destination, night had fallen. Being surrounded again by multiple storeys, having come from the utmost of rural areas, felt like a dream. Brands that I recognised, and many that I didn't, surrounded me. The hostel I had planned to arrive at was off by a few streets. Trooping through the narrow back-roads at night, the peace and warmth of the evening comforted me. I found my place of refuge, paid for a few nights, dumped the bag, and set about trying to locate some food.

Finding a few nearby students, I asked if they knew of anywhere to eat, and was directed to a small restaurant still open. A simple meal of soup, rice and *pide* later, I grabbed a dark, grainy photo of a bridge across the city, to let friends and family back home know that I'd made it in. Walking back, away from the main roads, I was alone again. Nothing but the calming rhythm of boot on tarmac echoed off the streets of Eskişehir.

Days 19 – 22: '(Young) Old City'

Resting in Eskişehir
19th – 22nd Oct 2021

The hostel was quieter than I had expected, or hoped for. I encountered a Moroccan girl, and a couple cycling from France to Turkey, but my hopes of building up a larger group to explore the area with were frustrated. Wandering throughout the town, however, I felt rejuvenated. I felt alive again, as if I had wandered back into a different version of normal life. Taking the opportunity to re-calibrate, I took refuge in the coffee shops overlooking Eskisehir's canal, borrowing their WiFi to update the social media accounts of my progress, plan potential routes and timelines for the next stage, transfer over money, and work out what I needed to resupply. As well as trying to find new warm kit for the nights, there was plenty of replenishing to do.

I also got in touch with the producer of *Fair Enough*, and we discussed the possibility of actually coming onto the show to speak about the trip. Getting the Adelaide – Turkey time zones to align wasn't easy, but I was excited at the idea of being able to tell the story so far to a wider audience. At any rate, my fleeting interactions with the Fairbairn brothers were one way of measuring how much time had elapsed, as the third week of this strange new lifestyle rolled around.

The main problem I sought to tackle, however, was how to deal with future encounters with dogs. It was a question I had pondered extensively since the first incident. A firearm was, sadly, out of the question. Any form of large knife or machete would have felt reassuring to carry. However, doing so would have sent very much the wrong signal to people I was relying on to trust me at first glance, particularly in urban areas where I'd spend a not-insignificant amount of time. Eventually, having sought some local advice, I settled on a squeeze bottle of *kolonya*,[12] and a small metal hammer. The former was based on someone's second-hand experience of deterring dogs with a spray of water, so I hoped that the alcoholic *kolonya* would be more effective. The hammer would do damage at arm's length, if I needed it to, but could also put in tent pegs, and looked less threatening than a knife. It weighed a ton, and was probably excessive. If only for my own reassurance, though, I felt the need to carry something.

---

[12] A scented, highly alcoholic liquid (often around 80%) used as a fragrance since Ottoman times, and since 2020, as a readily available hand sanitiser. Helpful for staying hygienic, lighting fires, deterring dogs, and smelling good.

Eskişehir was a beautiful little city to spend some needed resting-up time in. It was a stunning place to wander round, idling along the main river's wide boulevards, watching the world go by. Founded three thousand years ago, the 'main strip' thronged with students and young people, yet felt refreshingly less tourist-oriented than İstanbul. As modern as the city largely felt, the old town in the city's southern side was still made up of tiny streets and traditionally styled houses, which I spent hours wandering through, absent-mindedly enjoying the aesthetic of the built environment.

Whilst strolling down the main high street, I found an advert for 'Happy's English speaking café', for folk wanting to practice their English speaking. Intrigued, I visited the place, and was greeted by an extremely enthusiastic man, who promptly introduced himself as 'happy'. I tried to clarify his name, but apparently that was it. After a little confusion, I explained to him that the Turkish name *Mutlu* (happy) isn't used literally in English, and that there aren't many men with the name 'happy' in England. He wasn't overly 'happy' to hear this, but nevertheless offered me accommodation, food, or just about anything else I could need whilst there, and invited me to spend as much time as I could at his café. He ran structured sessions for students in particular, as well as hosting general meetups and one to one sessions.

So, one evening, still kitted out in walking boots, olive green trousers, a walking shirt, a lightweight bodywarmer and the beginnings-of-a-beard from a fortnight of not shaving, I rocked up. I was greeted by ten or so confused students, and their teacher, a native Russian. We started on an exercise about our families and friends, in scenes reminiscent of my own halting attempts at secondary school French. I provided a few examples, working hard to try and remain understandable to students who were about as confident in English as I was in their language. I was never sure whether it was politer to speak my own language to a non-confident speaker, or to try their language, and do so dreadfully. I immediately became a fascinating character to them and exchanged a lot of contact details that evening. I would keep up correspondence with a few particular characters throughout the journey. I made the time to hang out with a few other new-found friends from Couchsurfing, who showed me a little more of Eskişehir's nightlife.

The plan for Stage Two was fairly simple. A single road lead from Eskişehir to the next city, Afyonkarahisar (or Afyon). There seemed to be only flat terrain to cover. My original start date was the 22nd of October. However, ever true to form, I groggily realised at 10:30 that morning that any sort of real progress that day was not going to happen. I had a half-day, walking my belongings over the far south side of the city, and moved into a small hotel on to allow for better tidings the next day. I noted the location for next time I would be back in Eskişehir. With my new-found friends in the city, there certainly would be a next time.

4: The firefighters of south Sakarya. Tea not pictured.

5: Abandoned railway bridge across the Sakarya.

6: Ozur.

7: The remains of breakfast, Kızılkaya.

8: The two teachers in Kızılkaya. 30+ over-excitable children not pictured.

9: Geyve, looking south into the hills. The trail beckoned.

10: Yusuf's house (under construction), Alıplar. The photo was taken from his workman's shed, where we sheltered.

11: Taking stock on the ascent, Alıplar.

12: My hosts in Çime. Mischievous cat not pictured.

13: Two good friends, Köprücek.

14: My spot in the centre of Köprücek.

120

15: My hosts in Köprücek. Troublesome cats not pictured.

16: The hostel owner lending a hand with route planning, Gölpazarı.

17: Pack-less, atop the un-named hill, south of Gölpazarı.

18: Entering Büyükbelen.

19: Mustafa's tea shop.

20: Büyükbelen by night.

21: Sunrise, Büyükbelen.

22: The interior of Mustafa's house.

23: 'My' room at Mustafa's.

24: Mustafa himself. To this day, the most enthusiastic salesman of pekmez known to man.

25: On the move, north of Yakacık.

26: Stopping to rest feet and recharge, north of Yakacık. In isolated segments, solar charging stops became more important.

27: The gang.

28: Making acquaintance with a local, post resupply (film).

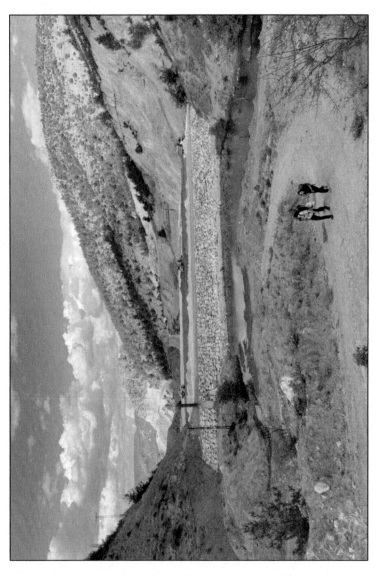

29: Traversing the dam, en route to Hisarcık. The concrete support pillar on the left made a useful handrail.

30: Hisarcık by dusk. The calls to prayer of mosques dotted through the valleys carried further in the cool evening.

31: Pausing to take stock, south of Hisarcık (film). As a consequence of bringing friends, the vast majority of photos actually featuring me come from those 48 hours.

32: Waxing boots, south of Hisarcık (film).

33: Cait and the old woman, Ortaca.

34: Leaving the clouds, en route to Uludere.

35: Backgammon, Uludere.

36: A lesson in menemen preparation (film), Uludere.

37: Alara. North of Eskişehir.

38: Central Eskişehir.

39: Odunpazarı, Eskişehir.

Stage Two

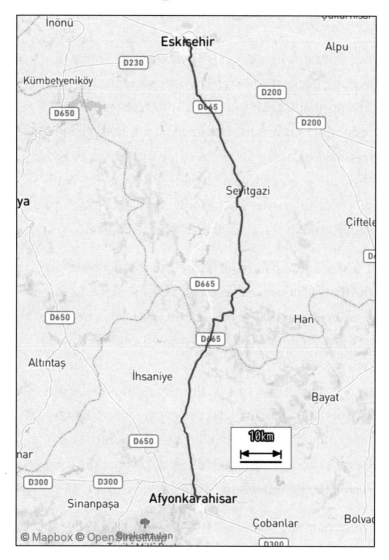

Eskişehir – Afyonkarahisar

Day 23: 'Departing paradise'

Odunpazarı, Eskişehir – Patch of grass, Akpınar
23rd Oct 2021

Leg 2 began with a generous helping of *menemen* in a sleepy café, nestled in the cosy streets of the old town. The portion was far too small for the energy I'd be needing, but it was too late once I'd finished. The place was deserted, save for me. A sign hung on a wall, asking *"how are you"*, surrounding the words *"I'm fine"* with scores of adjectives. I could only translate a handful, but understood the 'live laugh love' vibe regardless.

Tacking hard up into the hill on which Odunpazarı sat, the first challenge was to break out of the city. Early on, the sun came out in force. The steep incline out of the city proved more challenging than I'd envisaged, and I was glad I'd left a whole day to get clear of the city. As sure as night followed day, the pleasantries of the old quarter faded into endless construction site, rolling tarmac and half-finished buildings. Crossing the odd house's backyard, I was finally spat out onto the main road linking Eskişehir to Afyon.

The monotony of endless road began again. Although it felt satisfying to have cleared the boundary to the city, and be making progress again, it was hardly the sort of space to write home about. Later that afternoon, whilst having lunch at a park-type picnic area, a few men came over to join me. They handed over piles of snacks for the journey, and watched me wolf down some tinned tuna and bread with an oddly invested fascination. The sun started to seriously get to me after a while: walking ever-south, I was constantly walking directly into its glare, and there was little cover on the barren side of the road. As before, the long, empty stretches of highway with no end in sight were some of the most mentally challenging periods of the journey to cover. The constant contact with hard tarmac, with little to distract from the monotony or dull aches, took a lot out of the day. For breaks, there was little cover, aside from the lone pines lining the road. The day passed uneventfully.

Around halfway, I set a goal to get to a tiny village denoted on the map as Akpınar. Entry into the village was near silent, but I was simply grateful to have made it in on time. It was little more than a few homes and sheds for cattle, sitting on a gentle hill up towards a mosque. Mercifully, the village's small corner shop was still open, with plentiful fresh food that I enjoyed for one more day. Stopping over at the mosque to find water, I spoke to a man tending to the mosque's garden, to ask if I could pitch somewhere. I presumed he was the imam. He pointed to a patch of short grass in the centre of the village. As I set up, the couple whose house I had settled adjacent to looked on, confused. Once or twice, their cat came out to enquire about my presence, but each time grew bored, and scampered back under their gate to its owners. This bizarre routine wasn't easy yet, but I felt that at least I could rest for the day.

Having gone through the rest of the motions for setting up camp, I returned to the mosque to fill up some water to cook with. Returning, a herd of cows had appeared, from somewhere, and were trooping slowly down the lane towards my tent. As they moved sullenly along the track, I awkwardly tip-toed around the herd. They began grazing on a scrawny patch of dried, overgrown grass, just over the road from where I had made camp. Their owner, content that his herd were eating their fill, came over and introduced himself. He had also come from Afghanistan, but I couldn't understand where exactly, or when he'd arrived in Turkey. I offered him some of my bread, as staying in his village (or at least, on ground that he grazed his cows on) felt right. When the same cat from earlier came begging again, my new friend stomped near it to scare it off, advising me to do the same. I enjoyed my own meal of pasta, fresh cheese and bread, as he drove his cattle out into the barren, bitingly cold night.

Day 24: 'Papers, please'

Patch of grass, Akpınar – Mosque, unnamed village near Sarayören
24th Oct 2021

I waited to leave on Day 24, letting the sun's warmth burn off the morning's dew and charge the devices. It made a pleasant contrast to the freezing night before, the additional warm kit I had since acquired doing very little to keep the bitter night out.

The only break in the day's monotony came at lunch. A seemingly nice, upmarket restaurant lay halfway along the day's route. As much I was becoming wary of relying on Maps for the actual 'ground truth', fortunately this one happened to exist. Why it stood out in a field, 20-minutes by car from anywhere, was beyond me. The manager was lovely, and after the usual 'where are you from' introduction, insisted on practicing his English with me. A few more families came and went, evidently bemused by the sweaty traveller who was sat adjacent to a pack taller than him. I had something spicy involving lamb, and far, far more starters than I had bargained for.

The afternoon was another monotonous slog. The same unbroken exertion, on an unforgiving surface, with little stimulation to distract from the constant low-level pains, was becoming more mentally draining than I had first factored for. It only reinforced to my mind that staying on a main road for the entire trek would be unbearable, and that I needed to get away from such routes later in the trek. Seeing a cluster of houses off to my right, I assumed I had arrived at Sarayören, and dismounted the highway to approach the tiny settlement. Having since retraced my route, the tiny grid of houses could not have been Sarayören, and I have no idea what the name of the village was. Regardless, upon arriving, a passing driver recommended I try near the mosque for somewhere to camp.

On doing so, I met a man focused on repairing part of the building, sweating over planks of wood he was cutting. Dressed in casual work clothes and trainers, and not looking too far over 30 years old, I presumed he was a volunteer or workman. He was happy for me to sleep inside the walls of the grounds, so long as I was in view of several cameras at the front of the building. I suggested just pitching outside the walls of the mosque's compound, but he rejected this idea, citing something about dogs that I didn't quite pick up. After trying unsuccessfully to pitch on the brick courtyard, under a camera as requested, the man took pity on my efforts, and let me into a room inside the lower level of the mosque. I was tremendously grateful for somewhere warm and dry, although the room's large, curtainless windows, felt oddly exposed.

Far from just a workman, I eventually worked out that the man was the mosque's imam, who lived in a small home in the grounds of the mosque with his family. That evening, his seventeen-year-old son brought over a cup of tea and a delicious sandwich, inquisitive as to who I was, and we chatted. The conversation was cut short, however, by the arrival of a loud, confident man, who burst into the room after the Imam's son. After welcoming me to the village, he introduced himself as the village 'leader' and asked to take a photo of my passport. I was reluctant to hand it over, but there was nothing I could do. Sure enough, nothing malign happened, but I couldn't understand the difference in reception between this village and other places I'd been to. Eventually, as I was drifting off to sleep on the green felt sofa, it dawned on me that I'd passed a large prison complex the day before, which probably made an unaccompanied male walking by the roadside a little more suspicious than usual.

Day 25: 'Ghost towns'

Mosque, unnamed village near Sarayören – Santral Park Campsite, Seyitgazi
25ᵗʰ Oct 2021

Getting up and away early, for once, paid off. Having electric light in the dark mornings, and a solid wall between me and the rest of the world, was fantastic. Warm water in the early morning from the mosque's solar water heater, kept for washing before prayer, made a nice change from the wet wipe washes I was used to otherwise. I departed early in the hope that the next shop on the journey existed for breakfast. Not wishing to wake my hosts, I left a postcard expressing my thanks to the imam and his family. His son later reached out via social media, and I asked that he thank his father from me once more.

It was a bitterly cold morning. I never walked wearing layers, but came close to wishing I had done so for the first fifteen minutes of the day. The shop I'd been relying on for breakfast didn't exist, so 'breakfast' that day consisted of a packet of excess emergency rations that I'd grown sick of carrying. I kept moving to try and stay warm, getting straight back on the road after wolfing down the sparse food, and hoped the next advertised establishment would exist.

It didn't. I found a village instead that, although clearly lived in and occupied, felt deathly quiet. The residents were, for whatever reason, entirely absent. The café I had planned to eat at was there, but closed, as if for the winter. I settled down in the courtyard of another mosque to cook up three packets of noodles. Sat on a cinderblock behind a low wall to keep out of the wind, wrapped in layers to keep the bitter breeze out, the whole scene felt uncanny. Only a stray dog padded the lanes between houses, and even the highway remained near silent.

I pushed on. Even though I was moving, and the dark overcast skies kindly refrained from raining, the biting wind stripped away the heat, and I found myself upping my pace to maintain a semblance of warmth. As morning turned to afternoon, and the afternoon wore on towards the evening, the clouds cleared, and a blindingly bright sun became punishing to walk into again. Towards the end, a powerful, dull ache engulfed my feet. Eventually peeling off the motorway, the apparent absence of accommodation in the town of Seyitgazi persuaded me to try a campsite instead, which lay on a shortcut to my route for the next day. I paused, as a dense heard of goats was driven along the road. Two dogs padded along behind, obediently. The last stretch took me through tiny lanes, tractors bringing their harvests in as the sun set slowly.

I finally reached the fence-line of my campsite, nearing exhaustion, to find the gate padlocked. There was no way it could be climbed, so I set my pack down, and began jogging along as much of the fence line as I could access. Trying in several places to break through and climb in, the foliage proved too dense all around. I was stuck. Rerouting and coming back the way I had come would take hours, over kilometres, and there might not be anyone on the other end. The sun setting, in desperation I followed the fence line around back the way I had come, and began pushing through hedges and over fences to keep close to it. Wading a stream, the fence line finally turned. Walking straight through the centre of a field, no longer with the energy to look for the path, I had arrived.

It was staffed by a few men, although at this time of the year I was their only guest. Paying far too much for a spot to stay on, for the first time since arrival, I pitched on an actual, legitimate campsite. Dinner was a meal of freshly baked *pide*, mine and the resident staff the only ones eating that evening. We huddled around a log fire: I updated my journal and texted my new-found friends in Eskişehir, as they lit cigarettes on the flames of logs, and chatted in low tones. The night was desperately cold. Adding layers around midnight did little to help, and I could do little else but pull the sleeping bag more tightly around my black woolen hat.

Day 26: 'The Longest Day'

Santral Park Campsite, Seyitgazi – Midas Han Project, Çukurca
26th Oct 2021

The morning, like the night, was horribly cold. Although it felt inconsequential at the time, waking and leaving as late as I had left it would have a dire effect that day. Breakfast was an expensive platter of traditional Turkish food, which I doubt would have cost as much had I not obviously been a foreigner.

My plan for the day had changed after my experiences of the last two days of highway wandering. Instead of persisting in the hard shoulder of some provincial road, I planned to hike up into the hills through some smaller villages. Although it involved more elevation gain, the new route was slightly shorter. Furthermore, as much as I no longer trusted Maps to give me the whole ground truth, there appeared to be a hotel with genuine, positive, recent reviews along the way, despite sitting in a tiny, obscure village called Çukurca. I decided to risk it, as much to escape the dull monotony of the last few days as to save time. So, as I left the campsite, I took a sharp turn left, and left behind tarmac and grass for the thick, dry, chalky dust of the track. As I passed a field of women picking tomatoes, each stood up to watch my progress, too far for me to greet, but close enough for them to watch me pass by.

It wasn't far before a rash-like pain slowly took over my lower back. The pack, fastened tightly around my waist to keep the load on my hips, dug my belt into my skin, and rubbed painfully as I walked on. My feet had already begun to play up, and so I stopped a few kilometres in at the first bus shelter. I reapplied foot tape, despite only having done so an hour before, and let the warm, dry air flow over my back. Some men appeared, and jokingly insisted on trying on the pack. Although they were taken aback by how heavy it was, the pack fortunately survived the encounter.

The surface of the dirt track wound around small hills, on a steady but noticeable incline. It was mostly compacted, dusty gravel, which would get into my lungs whenever a breeze or passing truck would stir some up. Pausing at some ancient stone sheep huts, I realised just how long the day was going to be.

The same sensation arose at the crest of an incline. I looked out into miles and miles of flat, exposed plane, and despaired. The only recognisable feature between the sky and the rolling scrubland was the track I would be walking on, which vanished over the horizon, dizzyingly far away. The occasional truck would traverse the barren landscape, and a long cloud of dust would drift across the plane in its wake. When I would ask about places to resupply, each driver would reply *"no market"*, almost in disbelief that I had asked. Having left the shelter of the small hills behind, the burning sun was accompanied by a bitter wind, which stripped away any residual warmth and whipped dust into my face. Simultaneously burning in the sun and chilled by the wind, the skin of my face began to take a beating.

I can't recall what exactly began the cycle, but a severe spiral of negative thoughts began to overtake me. *There was nothing here for miles on end, and you're already exhausted? Who else would do something as stupid as this? You did – and now you're not even able to achieve it yourself?* Often in other contexts, when working hard or training physically, I find it frustrating to have someone tell you to keep going, to lean in and to carry on, as if I am not already doing so. Yet, with no anchor in the form of a friend, coach or team, I felt my frustration mounting uncontrollably fast, and the cycle of negative thinking begin, picking up speed. Knowing myself, I understood that stopping to rest would only lead to more wallowing, and more irrational despair. And so, I plodded on.

At the next village, again, there was no sign of life anywhere. Settling down at 13:00, pain had spread to the front of my right food, under where my laces were tied day on day. Desperate for shelter from the sun and wind exposure, I crouched in behind a narrow wall next to the cemetery to rest, pulling on layers and doing my utmost to stay out of the freezing wind. Concerned at this new pain, I mentioned it to Lucy, who (after consulting Google) suggested that it could potentially be a serious issue. Her advice was to immediately rest it, and go no further that day. *As if that was an option!*

My anger and frustration from the day were replaced by a low drumbeat of worry. As I prepared a dried camping meal of beef and rice stew, left to me by Jack and Cait, a general dread that maybe I had bitten off more than I could chew enveloped me. If I had indeed hit a limit, I could not have chosen many worse places to do so. My intended destination was still fourteen kilometres away, which was far enough to make me think about contingency plans. If I couldn't make it, I would have to hope the next village along was more populated that this one. If it wasn't, then I'd deal with that then.

Resolved to go as far as I could, and deal with what happens next later, I made some preparations. Adjusting the straps on my pack to realign the weight, I fastened a *shemagh*[13] around my face to keep the skin from being burnt by the sun and wind further. It was clear I couldn't continue walking in boots. Lucy advised me to try walking in sandals. I had initially scoffed at the idea, but with little options left, I had a go. My motivation now was less to finish the day, and more to simply get out of there.

To my surprise, the sandals worked. I was lucky that I had brought a pair of thickly padded, sturdy, well-made sandals back in Geyve, rather than trying to walk in my first pair of cheap flip-flops. The chalk dust on the road felt cool around my worn, tired toes, and although walking on stony ground was challenging, I could keep to the flatter parts of the track most of the time. The sandals rubbed and blistered in their own ways, but they let the air circulate over my feet, and vitally took the pressure off my right ankle for a period. I was moving slowly, but moving. I made a final, brief stop in a woodblock to make a change of trousers, which seemed to relieve some of the rubbing on my back. It was now just a matter of keeping on going. A few kilometres on, and the track passed through more woods, before rolling back into a valley. The winds thus died down, and the sun became less intense as it set. As calming as the scene was, it was an

---

[13] A square of woven fabric, worn in various parts of the Middle East.

153

uncomfortable reminder of how late it was getting.

Şükranlı, the last village before Çukurca, sat in a small valley, the fields aside used for grazing. I arrived at roughly the same time I would normally want to have a tent up by, the light rapidly receding. Whilst taking on some Kendall Mint Cake, reserved for the most exhausted of situations, I debated what to do next. The safe option was to curtail my plans and ask around for a spot to pitch in where I stood, which was safer but would have consequences for tomorrow's travels. The other, knowing that a warm bed and a proper square meal potentially over the next few hills in Çukurca, was to press on through the darkness of early evening. I welcomed the idea of proper rest, to let my feet ease back in. At the same time, the remaining five kilometres to Çukurca lay entirely empty. At the midpoint, I would be two kilometres from either settlement, in pitch black, on a road that I had seen one vehicle pass along since five that afternoon. The prospect of twisting an ankle, suffering some other minor injury, or encountering anything (or anyone) out there, with no prospect of help, was not attractive.

I decided to risk it. Calling ahead to make sure that the place existed, my basic conversation skills struggled again to work out if they had a room, but eventually managed. I couldn't be sure, but the voice on the other end mentioned something about food, which I agreed to wholeheartedly. I said I would be there in an hour. I could work out the details later. I untied my boots for the sides of pack, where they had been hung for the last nine kilometres, and pulled them on over my still-damp socks. I dug out a torch to hold in one hand for emergencies, and holding the two walking sticks loosely in the other, I set off into the blackness.

Wanting to be off the road and out of the night as quickly as possible, I doubled down. Covering the downhill and flatter segments at a light jog, as fast as I could sustain for a few minutes at a time, kept me warm as the last of the light faded. I ran as much as I felt safe to over the occasionally uneven ground, and as much as my body could put up with. Although my feet held up, my back bitterly complained. With each jolt and jump, more of the skin was rubbed off by the heavy pack. Tightening the straps to pull it up off my hips only fatigued my upper body faster, and letting it sit on my hips now sent sharp pangs when it touched a spot rubbed raw. Alternating between the two became the best way to cope. Whatever else was hurting was balanced against the distinctly uncomfortable feeling of being far from help. After the first couple of kilometres, I slowed to a quick stride, to avoid making more noise than needed, and to stay alert. I hoped that whatever lay out in the night wouldn't happen to cross the road as I did.

In the moonlight, the white chalk track stood out from the sea of blacks and greys making up the surrounding fields. The dark spots of rocks, shrubs, and tree stumps seemed to move if I focused on them too heavily, morphing into crouched silhouettes, low-moving animals, or any number of strange, insidious shapes. Highly strung, scanning for the slightest sound or movement, I felt alert. I had settled into a quick, strong march. The cool night's air sat still, and nothing punctuated the silence save my boots in the dust. Although loath to stop, given my fear of any slight noise at this point, I couldn't help but marvel at the stars stretched out above. The north star sat directly behind me, hanging over the route I had travelled that day, and the hundreds of kilometres I had covered so far. As much as I was strained to any noise that might break the silence, about halfway through the blackness, I felt a moment of genuine peace.

The road passed its final bend, and up ahead the silhouette of a minaret stood out. I breathed a little more easily. Coming up past the sign for Çukurca, the smell of wood-smoke and the mild chill brought back strange memories to winters evenings in England. Taking a right into the village, illuminated only by a scarce few streetlamps, I hoped desperately that this well-rated hotel, in a village with no market, one mosque, and a population probably in the low hundreds, really existed. Reaching the end of the last street, I saw a sign, reading 'Midas Han'. It did.

I was loudly greeted at the gate by an enormous *kangal*.[14] Bounding up to the gate at full pace, the animal took a sniff at the back of my hand, and was promptly content to slink quietly back inside. I touched down at 19:30, exactly an hour after sunset. I was welcomed in by the same woman who I had spoken to previously via phone, and shown to small, wood-fire lit room, in what seemed to be a converted stable. Dumping my pack and donning two fleeces, I crossed through their small, enclosed courtyard to the main lodge, where a meal of thick soup, lamb, and vegetables was waiting. Having eaten my fill, I returned to my room, threw a last log on the fire, and slept deeply.

---

[14] A large, powerful breed of dog, native to the mountains of Turkey.

Day 27: 'That belongs in a museum'

By the time I awoke, the room was icy cold. Breakfast was a traditional Turkish meal, of a variety of breads, sausage, cheese, fresh honey, and tomatoes, with plenty of *çay*. Looking out of a window over the wide, flat landscape, I could make out the façade and columns of an ancient tomb, cut into the rock of the shallow, wide valley. I had been given a guide to the local archaeological sites on arrival, written by a Dutch archaeologist who had mapped and documented many of them. After breakfast, whilst I was enjoying planning a short stroll over to explore, a large, jovial-looking man with a thin white beard walked into the dining room, and introduced himself with an unfamiliar European accent.

Ben Claarkson was a friendly host, if characteristically blunt for a Dutch person. Upon explaining (in English, for the first time in a while) what I was doing, I was taken aback by his response: he replied, simply, "ah, that sounds similar to what I did". We spent the next few hours swapping stories of our respective efforts to traverse Turkey, what had driven us to undertake them, and how we two foreigners had found ourselves in the silent, ancient valleys of central Anatolia. He had completed a report on his own journey across Turkey, taking a number of his Turkish students with him from when he taught at Ankara University. Reading through his notes, his military experience as a former forward observer in the Dutch Army came across strongly. I recognised many of his 'lessons learnt', and was relieved to see that it wasn't just me who had become fully reliant on pasta and mosque-drawn water. His own adventure had taken significantly less time than I had planned for mine, partially down to the native Turkish speakers who came with him, and partially because he had found a route shorter than mine by 30 kilometres. This was most frustrating. I thought I had done quite well on that front.

He explained that he had set up the hotel out here with a fellow archaeologist (who I'd met that morning) after documenting many of the Phrygian, Roman and Byzantine sites surrounding us. Having become an academic authority on the region through fieldwork and study, it was now his intent to make the valleys in the region, collectively home to thousands of years of history, accessible to more people. I was also formally introduced to the *kangal*, called Clara, that morning. Having evidently learnt my name, she was very affectionate, despite our first encounter. The only interruptions to her lazing in the sun that morning was to chase cats off the premises, or to try and escape whenever Ben or I opened the gate out onto the open landscape. As much as I ought to have settled down for the day and rested, Ben had wet my appetite for exploring this unique little corner of the country. I had hardly planned to go off exploring ancient ruins, but having spread my freshly-washed clothes out to dry on a bench in the sun, I packed a day-bag, and set off through the fields.

Slowly wandering through the layers of history on display was the perfect antidote to the bitter preceding day. Any doubt I had entertained over whether this detour had been worth it was immediately dispelled. Drifting through thousands of years of accumulated history was something of a cathartic relief. Sitting in caves that had been homes for hundreds of years, some populated far more recently than ancient times, I listened to the herds of semi-wild cattle migrate across the valley. As the sun began to dip, I climbed up onto the great worn rocks, riddled with caves, tombs and inscriptions, and gazed out over the gently rolling landscape. The moment was somehow made more beautiful by how unplanned this whole part had been. Not only had I made progress. I had discovered something truly worth finding as well.

I met a few others also exploring, as local guides took couples from Ankara and Palestine around on tours. At dinner, I encountered another couple visiting the area:

around a roaring fire, Ben and us all exchanged English and Turkish lessons. Having put off doing so, I packed late into the night, listening to the soft tunes of a playlist sent to me from a friend in Eskişehir.

Day 28: 'Grab a patch of steppe'

Midas Han Project, Çukurca – Roadside, Gökbahçe
28ᵗʰ Oct 2021

I rose early. Paying for my stay was more difficult than I anticipated, and Ben (very kindly) took on trust that my payment would go through in the three working days the bank promised. After we grabbed a few photos together, and I had worked out how another of Ben's sketch maps aligned to satellite pictures and Maps, I set off. I made excellent progress over the mostly open ground, with only one minor dog encounter to speak of. They kept their distance as I took a dried streambed down through a progressively steeper valley, once more far from any real route. I passed a few more remarkable archaeological sites, such as some underground sheep-pens from the Phrygian era, still providing cool shade for a few rabbits thousands of years after being dug. It wasn't long before I was back on an actual track, which would take me back onto my original route soon enough.

Yapıldak was the first small village with a shop on route. A group of inquisitive men, arms held behind their backs as typical, enquired as to where I had come from, and were bemused by my answer. Nevertheless, the elderly shopkeeper himself was very kind. Him, his wife, and I sat around and enjoyed bread and tea, whilst a large, old

TV chattered away distantly about the state of Turkey's economy. My hosts both remarked how well *"sterlin"* was doing. After this quick lunch, the road wound around thickly wooded hills, back towards the main south-bound road to Afyon I planned to jump back onto. The only real highlight was a child, not older than 14, learning to drive a tractor along the middle of the road.

Gökbahçe was a village on the intersection of my track and the main highway. As the track banked West, the setting sun became dazzling, only relenting as it dipped below the next hillside's tree-crested ridge. Approaching the village, a friendly shepherd joined me to cross a small bridge over a brook. He handed me a few small, crab-apple like fruits, which I found to be incredibly sour. He smiled, and I left him to the challenge of crossing his flock across the main road. I came to a small building on the side of the highway, which had been extended out with plastic sheeting and wooden beams. A family sat around, and I asked if there's anywhere to stay nearby. Confused, they said no, but after seeing that I was happy to camp on the empty steppe adjacent to them, they waved me on and watched, curious as got the tent down.

Struggling to realise what it is I'm looking at, I eventually understood that the extended shack was, in essence, a motorway service station. I called in to see what food they could offer, and enjoyed some light *gozleme*[15] and *çay*, sitting under a makeshift plastic awning. As the woman serving me came to understand what I was up to, her mood lightened. I asked why a stove sat out by the road, the several kettles of brewing tea sending clouds of steam into the cold evening. It took time for me to understand, but I eventually grasped that the roadside stove was a canny advertisement for their small café.

I was about to leave before a pair arrived, who invited me to join them for even more *çay*. One was a teacher in Eskişehir, who warned me that Afyon wouldn't be as warm and welcoming as the rest of my journey, for some reason. It turned out he knew a little about the Phrygian valley I'd just passed through. Most of his response went over my head, but I also gleaned that he was into his history of the First World War. Having done my own undergraduate dissertation on the Great War, I was more than a little overjoyed to spend a few minutes flicking through his social media, which documented his collection of memorabilia and decorations from the Ottoman and German empires.

After my final dose of *çay*, I was offered a lift to a nearby

---

[15] Light, savoury flatbreads. Needing the calories, I ordered a few.

bakkal[16] for some more supplies. I thought the place was close by, but halfway through the car journey I panicked that I'd effectively abandoned my tent, valuables and all. By the time I'd stopped flapping, and worked out how to explain *"my passport is in my tent this so too far please can we stop"*, we had arrived. I grabbed as much bread, cheese, coffee and other essentials, and got a lift back. All the gear was safe, my driver finding my flustered panic absolutely hilarious.

Once more, the night was cold enough to seriously struggle with sleeping. The thin roll-mat offered little insulation or protection from the ground, and I find myself developing deep, searing pains in my hips, as I tossed and turned throughout the night to ease the aches. Nothing worked.

---

[16] A simple shop, for daily essentials.

Day 29: 'Republic Day'

At 06:00, one of my first jobs was shaking the frost from the canvas, before the morning's sun would melt it and soak the tent through. As others awoke, I was waved over by a new couple at the service station. I chatted to Zeynep and her husband, and was told again that folk in Afyon were not as warm and welcoming as those in Eskişehir. I spotted that the stove we were all 'warming' ourselves around had written 'made in Eskişehir' on the side, and I made a surprisingly well received joke.

Delayed a little by the lovely conversation, I got onto the road as quickly as I could, conscious of the day slipping away. Once again, the twin aims of immersing myself in a new culture, meeting new people and pushing myself out of my comfort zone to build my language skills, clashed with the basic realities of life on the side of a road.

Starting the day in a thick fog, I was lucky that the Afyon – Eskişehir highway was at this stage a calmer, twin-lane road. For most of the day, I was gently climbing, before summiting the last set of hills, and dropping down over the watershed to the halfway point of the entire walk, and to Afyon.

It was only an hour or so in before I had to stop and pause to deal with feet issues. The problem now was not the underside of my feet, on the load-bearing edges or parts that rubbed, but on the surface of my toes where the leather of my boots folded into the flesh. The skin unhardened, I was having to clean, drain, wash, and dress these blisters as much, if not more often, than the others. If left unattended, they turned into sodden clumps of plaster, zinc oxide tape and woolen sock as the day progressed, carrying with them the risk of infection. As I rested, a shepherd tried to usher his flock across the road, with the help of his dog and family members. Along the rest of the journey, as the road wound around the hills and tracked the course of the gentle stream below, other shepherds guided their sheep along the steep verges, letting them graze between the mess of car detritus littering the edges of the road, and the valley below.

After finishing the morning's walk, and cooking myself a quick bowl of pasta in some stream-drawn water, the road widened out again, and I was stuck again on a multi-lane, concrete path. By early afternoon, I could feel my feet begin to seriously complain, in multiple places, but I pressed on. The prospect of being at the halfway point, of having effectively covered over half of the challenge, was an alluring prize. As I pushed on, once more stuck in the debris of a left-hand hard shoulder, it didn't occur to me that I would have to continue, for some distance, to reach anywhere to effectively 'come into land' and stay for the evening. I was dead-set on arriving at the halfway point.

Naturally, I missed it, so had to double back to find the rough area that corresponded with where Maps estimated halfway lay. It was difficult to be precise, but having a physical spot to symbolise the progress I'd achieved felt vital. The route would no doubt evolve as plans changed, but I had to mark how far I had come, somehow. Putting the pack down next to a lone tree, in an otherwise fully unremarkable field, and decided that I had made it.

I felt the same intoxicating cocktail of emotions as I had done in Geyve and Eskişehir. That heady mix of disbelief and euphoria that the whole adventure was actually happening was overpowering. If I had made it as far as fifty percent of the route, there was nothing that could possibly stop me from pulling through the rest. In my excitement, I carved my initials into a lone telegraph pole, leaving them barely legible in the cracked, dry wood. Turning to social media to put out a celebratory story, it was only then that I realised it was Turkey's Republic Day. I wished my small band of followers from the last 300 kilometres or so a good day. I had hoped to be in a major city by the time it rolled around, but that wasn't going to happen now. A few hundred metres away, a shepherd watched on as I remounted the pack, and limped back onto the highway.

It was only then, looking at the amount of ground to cover between 15:00 and sundown, that I began to mildly worry. If I could keep up a strident pace, I could at least reach somewhere with food and water before the sun dipped below the horizon. Starting late had, once more, left me racing the night. Thrashing myself harder than usual, to make it to 'halfway', would make that a more painful process than before.

Already beginning to dip towards the horizon, the sun cast lurid, beautiful shadows across the wild, ragged rocks and valleys to my east. To my west, the road had flattened out into yet another plateau, with another set of mountains adorning the far beyond. It was here, pacing it down the dead straight highway, that the pain began to truly mount. My belt began to cut into my sides again, and the numb over-arching ache that my feet had suffered with over the past few days became, for the first real occasion, acute. As time and exhaustion wore on, I searched the ground I was passing for a suitable pitch location, out of sight of the main road, and with any source of water. None appeared. I considered, not for a short while, finding refuge in any of the Phrygian caves that dotted the hills off to my left, but decided against it. It would be cold enough in a tent, let alone on a slab of rock open to the morning's frost.

The sun now clearly setting, and my other options for the evening having disappointed, I rejoined the race against the night. By now, my stride had shortened as I limped on, and I could only hope that a good night's sleep would let me continue the next day. Finally drawing in, with merely ten minutes until sundown, I reached the outskirts of Kayıhan. With little time to make introductions and risk being turned away, as night set in, I once again avoided being caught for want of permission. Off to the east lay nothing but empty dirt as far as the eye could see, dotted only by the occasional bush, with no one to complain of my presence. I threw the tent down in five minutes around 100 metres from the main road and the single line of houses opposite, but concealed by rocks and low-growing fir trees. As darkness took hold, I was wary of what lay beyond the pines behind the tent, and what might roam the empty wilderness at night. But those worries could wait. I was hungry.

I wrapped up in plentiful warm clothing, made careful note of the tent's location on W3W, and began walking into the village itself. Kayıhan was mostly a kilometre off the main highway, but the settlement had grown towards and around the road, giving me a few places to visit easily.

I had packed a small bag with some wash kit, should I be able to find anywhere to clean myself up, but I was mostly out to find as much food as I could.

My first stop was at a farm shop of sorts: wanting desperately to bring some variety to the usual pasta, bread, or cheese combination, I brought a large, fresh loaf of round bread, and a box of eggs. As I moved on, I arrived at the petrol station I had planned to grab a few light snacks from. To my delight, entirely unlisted on Maps, a bright, busy restaurant sat next to it. Starving, I wolfed down the largest portion of *izgara köfte* possible, and ordered some freshly made *pide* to take back with me, for good measure. A passing family, evidently midway through a wearisome journey somewhere, stared on at me. I tried to look friendly, but as I ate greedily, I was fighting a losing battle. In my black hat, fleece, stinking walking trousers and shaggy bits of beard, I didn't care.

Worried that my blisters could become infected, and to try and keep my feet vaguely hygienic, I set off for the village mosque. Turning west off the highway and towards the old village, I was stopped by a large, snarling dog. It displayed very little likelihood of letting me through. Knowing that sometimes it just took a bit of aggression to get them to take you seriously, I advanced on it a few times, yelling as loud as I dare, and swinging at its face with the stick. The dog was undeterred. I was considering how to handle this new challenge, when a passing car pulled over, blocking the dog off from me. I wandered on.

When I finally arrived at the mosque, the imam greeted me. He was another young man, like the imam back near Sarayören. He was an extroverted, enthusiastic character, who after keenly asking where I had come from, ushered me over to the mosque's washing station, and told me to take as much as I needed. This one, too, had warm water, which lifted off the layers of congealed dirt and sweat from my open blisters.

Once I was done, I wandered back into the thick darkness of the night. I was very glad that I'd got a fixed location code for the tent: although I was able to find it without much trouble, I'd have been stuck had I left the road and wandered into the wrong bush. Happy with how the evening had gone, I took a second to appreciate the unpolluted night sky, eating my warm *pide* as I watched the stars slowly drift across the empty black horizon. Surely, nothing could go wrong tomorrow.

Day 30: 'Breakdown'

Roadside, Kayıhan – Hotel, Gazlıgöl
30th Oct 2021

Another freezing night was concluded by another freezing morning. The tent was covered in a light dusting of frost, chunks of which fell down my neck as I emerged, blinking, into the bright morning. My plans for cold weather had fallen flat, completely, and I resolved (again) to get some better gear for the nights as soon as I could. My simple breakfast of boiled eggs and fresh bread wasn't as nice as I had hoped it would turn out. *They need salt*, I thought, sitting on the dirt whilst scooping out half-cooked yolk with hunks of crust.

Having packed down the tent, I sat back on the pack, and began administering copious amounts of foot tape. It was here that I first seriously doubted my ability to go on for the day, as I winced with each layer I wrapped around each slightly weeping sore. I tried to reason with myself. Afyon was twenty-eight kilometres away. That was only two days walk away, or potentially one if I thrashed myself as I had done before. It would take one last, full push, and I would be there. I was struggling to even get back onto the highway, but then I'd struggled yesterday. I did it then. I just needed to power through, and I could rest.

Reaching the petrol station to grabbed some more snacks, I accidentally interrupted a man praying as I walked in, so waited five minutes until he was done. As I hit the road out of village, the same dog from last night bounded up from the other side of the road, four lanes across. At first worried, given my lack of company, the dog tailed me for 100 metres, before getting bored and turning around. It escaped, without being hit by a car, or a stone of mine. I felt an odd wave of anger that it had gotten away, unscathed.

That frustration only mounted as I got going. The frosty morning turned to harsh, punishing sun, quickly. Stuck on the tarmac for the next twenty-eight kilometres, with nothing but empty ploughed fields either side and no appealing back-routes, the constant of the hard surface got seriously painful only an hour into walking. As much as I attempted to keep pressing on, and could have done so for longer, it was clear that today would not be going according to plan. My grand ambitions of pushing all the way to Afyon came thudding down to earth. I hobbled on for five or six kilometres, before beginning the search for somewhere to rest properly. My habit of irrational over-optimism when planning, particularly when up against my own deadlines, had come back to bite me once again.

The small town of Gazlıgöl was coming up ahead. The

whole place was little more than a collection of thermal baths and hotels, a cluster of squat concrete blocks, around some sort of thermal spring. They were scatted across the landscape as if thrown across haphazardly, sticking up from the soil like gravestones. The whole place felt like a motorway service station, that had grown far in excess of just fuelling cars, but had maintained the same foreboding sense of place-less-ness. It would have to do.

The distance covered was a severe downgrade from my plan, but that could look after itself. By 11:00, having covered off only a quarter of my normal day's progress, I finally staggered off the motorway, and limped up to the first place likely to have a bed for the night I could find. The man behind the desk of the first hotel asked for Ł500. This was about Ł400 higher than I was expecting, but I bit the bullet, being frankly unable to do anything else.

It was at this point that my card stopped working. Having been far from an ATM for the last few days, I had little cash to fall back on, and certainly not enough here. The receptionist had the great idea of going to a cashpoint nearby, which I agree to come with him to, leaving my pack in the care of a small child who I took to be his son. Expecting a short stroll round the corner, I imagined being able to hobble the distance, without the weight of the pack. After stepping outside, however, the man straddled a dirty, red, beaten-up trail motorbike, and beckons me to jump on the back. My attempt to ask for a helmet fell flat, and I could only articulate *"where head?"* a few times. This didn't land. So, entirely unprotected, I hopped on, and clung on for dear life. We mounted pavements, weaved in-between lorries, and crossed a few railways looking for a cashpoint that would work, but none of them did. I had the distinct feeling I was being taken for a ride, literally and metaphorically, but was utterly powerless to do anything else. I went with the flow.

Having exhausted all our options, I managed to convince him that I would transfer him the monies via banking app. After another round of wrestling with bank security features, he eventually accepts a screenshot of the transfer as proof. Having finally paid for a room, I was invited to join him and his wife for tea and pastries. A child asked what I was up to. Having got his answer, he moved onto the far more interesting question of how old I thought he was.

By around 14:00, I was finally left alone. I enjoyed a much-needed bath, and spent the afternoon keeping the weight off my feet as much as I could. My efforts to drain some of the most painful blisters were unsuccessful. The damage was simply too far below the surface of the skin, and I was unable to reach those that were really causing the trouble. Several sterilised needles and a little blood later, I gave up. I could rest properly tomorrow, if I could crack out one more long day to Afyon.

A little defeated, I lay down and texted a few contacts, to let them know of the delay and the lack of progress. A few moments later, a friend of mine from İstanbul texted me, pointing out that the handle of my travel Instagram had somehow made its way to Twitter, and seemed to be doing the rounds. She offered to help circulate it further, in case anyone she knew of could help along the rest of my journey. By the end of the day, quite literally hundreds of strangers had messaged, followed, and offered support of whatever I might need. They came from across Turkey and across the world, either offering hospitality or simply wishing me all the best for the rest of the trip. As much as the supportive messages of friends and family had previously meant a great deal, encouraging me to keep putting one foot in front of the other, it truly felt like there was a crowd behind me now. For a day on which everything seemed to have gone wrong, I was tremendously grateful.

I was twenty-four kilometres away. Normally that would be a long day. Given the state that I felt in, however, it felt enormous. I refused to worry about whether I could actually do it, and slept as early as my body would let me. Tomorrow, with this horrendous stage behind me, I could rest properly.

Day 31: 'The pain curve'

Hotel, Gazlıgöl – Afyon Polat Hotel, Afyonkarahisar
31ˢᵗ Oct 2021

The pain started immediately as I stepped out of the door, and back onto the dusty track running down onto the main highway leading south.

Naturally, I had completely forgotten that international bank transfers take three working days to process. I was lucky that the hotel manager was happy for me to leave unhindered. I promised to return and pay in cash if for whatever reason he hadn't got his money in three days' time, but hoped I'd never have to come back to this glorified service station of a town ever again.

The road wound through the last parts of Gazlıgöl. I was always frustrated whenever, confined to the side of another highway, I would be forced into the exact same wide curves and long stretches that were built for fast-moving vehicles. The sensation of being stuck in the outer lane of a running track, becoming ever more exhausted, pervaded. After six kilometres, I took my first break, crouching on the bench of a bus shelter, shivering in the stiff breeze as I took on chunks of chocolate and sipped water. As I got up, trying to move off again, boot leather dug into open, weeping sores, and stinging pains

179

shot through my feet. I staggered, leaning heavily on my staff, and stifled a shout. One foot at a time, the pack swaying side to side as I limped over the tarmac, I pushed on. Eight kilometres in, the road straightened out, and would carry on nearly due south for the rest of the day, and the rest of Stage Two.

Over the course of Day 31, I discovered that the pain of slogging onwards would follow something of a curve. Immediately setting off, the immediate sting of rubbed-raw skin and blister on tarmac would be nearly intolerable. As I would cover off the first kilometre or two, the pain would dull. I would get used to it. For three, four, five or six kilometres, I could plod on, and the discomfort would fade into the background. After six or seven, the discomfort would rebound. It would grow "gradually then suddenly". A dull pain could flare up in a few paces. I spent the day, for the most part, trying to stay at the bottom of the pain curve, marking the distance off in six-kilometre chunks, one by one.

Passing a petrol station, I encountered two kids, who looked around sixteen or so, walking the other way down the highway to Gazlıgöl. They explained they were taking a package to their father, and I explained I was walking to Antalya. We exchange amused, if bewildered pleasantries, the language barrier not stopping us from sharing the strange experience of walking in a country built around cars. Later, another rest stop took pace in the grounds of a domineering, newly built mosque. I took in the sight of kids playing, and a strange, loud, car-like vehicle drove past. It looked as if it were home-made, sheets of steel bolted onto a basic chassis like an overgrown Meccano project, and the several lads sitting in the open-top rear waved enthusiastically at me. I was left with more questions than answers.

Halfway to Afyon, I arrived in a small town called Çayırbağ, which sat either side of the main highway. Attempts to find a cooked meal fell flat, so I settled for a cheap lunch of bread and doner meat from the nearest supermarket. My feet had gotten no better, and the cold wind had picked up again. A few kids asked where I was from, and could scarcely believe my answer. One asked for me to say something in English, as if to prove my outlandish story. As they walked on, the loudest one in the group yelled, "goodbye!". I tried to look delighted back. Huddled next to the pack, I scraped bits of doner together with hunks of bread. What an enjoyable day it was.

The long, straight road to Afyon beckoned again. I was left with about eleven kilometres left to cover until I could properly rest. As the road stretched out, the transition back to rural, and once more into an urban setting, rolled through again. Fields of concrete, representing projects half-finished and half-abandoned, sprawled out, a grey band around the city. On the verge of the highway, old women harvested the shrubs which grew on the narrow green strip separating tarmac from field. They asked what I was doing, and I did likewise. I couldn't quite understand the answer, but in the surreal moment, our mutual well-wishing was wholly authentic.

A few more hours on, and I pass the first sign spelling out the city's name in full. I was greeted by an accommodation block for the city's university. An enormous, multistoried dormitory, it towered over the road, dwarfing everything and everyone, resembling more of a prison than accommodation for the innocent. Yet, passing it seemed to mark a threshold. I had crossed back into somewhere more alive, again. As I re-dressed my feet in the grounds of another mosque, politely ignored by the older men emerging from prayers, bustling flows of students hailed cabs and boarded buses. This was the last push in. I could feel my strength returning.

The last significant obstacle was a highway bridge. Just like outside Sakarya, where two intersecting highways met, the bridge that took my lane over and into the city narrowed, and my haven of the hard shoulder disappeared for a hundred metres or so. Standing at the roadside for a few minutes, it was clear that no safe opportunity to run into oncoming traffic would present itself. Crossing the road beneath me wasn't an option either, as tall fences along the central reservation precluded that. I was in no mood to turn around, and the effort I'd expended to reach this point weighed heavily on my appetite for risk. Crossing from the left lanes to the right, placing the flow of traffic behind me, I was in a better position to judge a good moment. Once it appeared, I leapt the metal barrier, and sprinted.

Leaning wholly into the decision to move, I dared not look back for a second. The pack jumped about on my back terribly, as if trying to escape. About halfway across the bridge, a motorcyclist pulled up and offered, frantically, a lift out of danger. With zero capacity to talk, I waved him on, shouting *"no thanks"* and running faster. Making it to the other side, he raised a hand to ask *"why?"*, but I was across. He bid a happy but confused farewell, and rode on. The whole thing took under twenty seconds, but felt as though it took an age. My body kicked me for doing so, and I slumped back into a poor-postured trudge on the other side, back in my hard shoulder.

Getting into the town itself, a light evening drizzle began.

I once more felt hugely out of place, my sweat-stained clothes and enormous pack clearly suited to somewhere other than normal, urban life. It was getting dark already, the cheap neon lighting of bars, supermarkets and cheap shops sparkling on the rows of rain-speckled windscreens. I meandered through taxis, sitting bumper to bumper around the narrow streets, and turning a last corner, arrived. I checked into a cheap room, which immediately smelt of cigarettes, and dumped my gear on the worn beige plastic chair.

A few minutes later, the manager re-appeared, and showed me into the neighbouring room. It took me ten minutes of nodding, asking for repetition and miming, but I eventually pieced together why I had been brought in here. He was trying to sell me an upgraded room, with a balcony. Not a chance. Balcony or no balcony, I wanted to sleep.

Days 32 – 34: 'Return to Eden'

Resting in Afyonkarahisar / Revisiting Eskişehir
1ˢᵗ Nov – 3ʳᵈ Nov 2021

Afyon certainly wasn't as bad as those who'd mentioned it before had made out. It was a historic city, defined by enormous rocks on which castles of old had been planted, looking down on the residents from on high. I was saddened that I didn't get to explore more and see them better, but my feet badly needed the rest. I was seriously concerned that I'd run into the same problems again when I set off for Stage Three, and so made it a priority to move around as little as possible. Once more, 'trekking' took precedence over 'travelling', and looking after my body in anticipation of the next stage had to take priority over exploring. It also rained constantly, and I had become strangely fond of staying warm and dry.

My main priority was getting a working local number again. A few days prior, before Gökbahçe, the tourist SIM card I had been using ran out of data, a month before I had expected it to do so. Replacing it proved an awful lot more difficult in Afyon than in İstanbul, where clearly marked *turist* SIM cards were available easily. It took a lot of failed attempts at speaking, and no doubt some very poor sentence structuring, but I eventually managed to buy a new SIM. Naturally it didn't work, and the morning was spent wrestling with tech, knowing that I had absolutely no hope of trying to enlist help over the language barrier. Eventually, I worked out that connecting to a remote hotspot from one phone with the other, and then changing a certain password mid-way through doing so would activate the connection, but only for a minute. It would have to do.

A day after arriving, the hotel owner texted me to say that his bank transfer "does not go". Unable to work out whether I had or hadn't paid him, and frankly not caring whether he got ₺500 or ₺1000, I took a *dolmuş* back to Gazlıgöl hotel with the cash, and some *baklava* to thank him for his patience. He was overjoyed, and after sharing some with me and his family, he gave me one last motorcycle ride back to the spot where the *dolmuşlar* departed from. I never saw Gazlıgöl again.

Having been invited to visit, I decided to spend a night back in Eskişehir, and getting the coach back over was a mostly smooth process. Going back would also allow me to pick up some better kit for the rest of the walk, some more gas for the stove, and other outdoors assortments that weren't to be found in Afyon. It was jarring to travel the same distance that had taken me a week's hard graft in a few hours, but reassuring to be back in a familiar place again. I was beginning to seriously like Eskişehir.

Stage Two was seriously hard work. If I had left Stage One thinking I could push myself a bit more, and cover some longer distances each day, Stage Two was a firm kick in the other direction. I was reminded, viscerally, that there was a limit as to just how much terrain I could manage in a day. I wasn't invincible. Stage Two would cast a long shadow over the rest of the journey, as a nagging reminder that seeing incredible places meant getting off the highways. Exploring Çukurca, a gem as beautifully pristine as it was hidden, was the firm highlight of Stage Two. It would serve as a reminder that the beautiful, the extraordinary, or the simply interesting were often found off the beaten track.

I threw together a crude plan as I packed late into the evening. Stage Three would involve less highways, because it would involve far less people. The intended destination was the town of Eğirdir, which sat on a huge lake with the same name, and had featured in Matt Krause's own tale of crossing Turkey from west to east. It was obvious that it would be a sparse, potentially lonely leg, simply from the geography. Despite all this, I knew I was over halfway. The emptiness of Stage Three would simply have to be the next challenge.

40: Afghan cow-herder and herd, Akpınar.

41: Straggling sheepdog comes to say hello, north of Seyitgazi.

42: The long road to Çukurca. The sheer size and magnitude of the empty plains made crossing a daunting task.

43: Carla.

44: The Midas Han tea

45: Shemagh donned, happy skin.

46: Playing Indiana Jones for a day, around Çukurca.

47: More sights around Çukurca.

48: Watching herds of cattle migrate in for the evening from a cave. Reportedly, some of the cave networks around the valleys were continuously occupied from the Phrygian era until the late 1960s.

194

49: The view southwards from Çukurca's treasures.

195

50: The halfway point.

51: Concealed from the road at Kayıhan.

52: ATM hunting via dirt bike, Gazlıgöl.

Stage Three

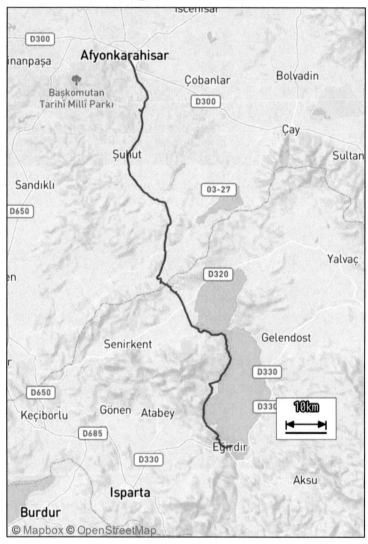

Afyonkarahisar – Eğirdir, Isparta

Day 35: 'Middle Lane Hogging'

Afyon Polat Hotel, Afyonkarahisar – Çeşme near Belkaracaören
4th Nov 2021

I checked out of the cheap hotel and left early, to try and get the distance necessary to get out of town. Only a few minutes in, I had to stop and repack to redistribute the weight around, to avoid being pulled over backwards by a misplaced tent. By this stage, more and more of my kit was not packed in the pack, but on, around, and attached to it. The whole haphazard mess hung together, karabiners and string hanging off at angles, I in turn looking progressively more dishevelled as the heap grew.

The transition from urban to rural was sharp, and the *dolmuş* were quickly replaced by tractors and the same homemade-looking cars I'd seen coming in. The path out of town was marked by constant construction. Walking through the furthest end of another road widening project, I saw that fresh tarmac had carved its way through a village. The demolition of houses on either side of the road could not have happened long before, as the remains of front gardens and the innards of homes lay fresh outside, exposed to the trickle of passing cars. Interior doors stood open to the world, now holding out the elements. I wondered what the residents had thought.

Leaving the city was hot, hard work. Without a hard shoulder, I crossed the main road multiple times to dodge the various concrete mixers and rollers making their way back towards Afyon. The day dragged on, through miles of half-formed construction sites and dumped rubbish at the side of the road. As in Sakarya, leaving towns was always the worst part. Cresting a hill, a lorry suffered a dramatic blowout as it rounded a corner, the scraps of tire only adding to the roadside detritus.

Eventually leaving behind the watershed that Afyon sat in, the route began a steep incline. At the foot of the first hill, I realised that, at least for now, the diggers and rollers had moved on, leaving a brand new three-lane highway entirely to myself. Although the steep incline was uncomfortable, progressing up the third lane of the new motorway was a luxury. Further on, diggers continued to break their way through the cliffs to build yet more lanes. One foreman crossed the road to ask what I was up to. Whilst his back was turned on the men he was supervising, three of them climbed into the bucket of a digger, and their mate picked them up, spinning them slowly, laughing. Across all creeds and cultures, blokes will be blokes, and heavy construction machinery is endlessly entertaining.

Not wanting to overdo the first day again, I came off the

highway at the next opportunity, straight through another construction site. Walking around tonnes of boulders being dumped from earlier, the workmen were nonplussed, and waved me through their chaos. I was trying to get close to the nearest village, Belkaracaören, to find a suitable spot for the night. Before I made it to the village proper, I came across one of the many freely flowing drinking fountains that dotted the landscapes, which I had come to know as *çesmeler* by now. With water access and a flat patch of ground, I promptly sacked off any plans to go any further.

Once I had the tent up, the sun began to slide below the smoothly rolling hills. As evening approached, the tranquil scene became a bustle of activity. Shepherds began to usher home their herds of sheep, goats, and cattle, which fanned out across the landscape like flocks of birds riding the wind. The distant sound of collar bells, sheepdog barks, and hoarsely yelled commands drifted down from the ridgelines, as if part of the very landscape. Driving their animals towards the village and past my tent, the shepherds themselves rode small donkeys, sitting forward on the animal atop fat leather saddles filled with kit. Letting their herds stop to drink from the same *çesme* I was reliant on, I approached a few to chat.

Two had what appeared to be large-calibre weapons,

either shotguns or large breech-loaded rifles. I asked what they were for, couldn't understand the answer, and let them get on their way. Knowing that the locals needed protection, or at least saw it necessary to carry it, put me on edge for the evening. To put my mind at least somewhat at ease, I hastily got a small fire going, and let it smoulder into the night as I retreated into the tent. Although a little on-edge, the spot was as good as any. Although I was only a kilometre from the highway, the stenches and sounds of the day's journey out of Afyon could not have felt further away.

Day 36: 'The last town'

Çeşme near Belkaracaören – Otel, Şuhut
5ᵗʰ Nov 2021

One of the same shepherds from the day before greeted me again in the morning, astride his donkey. The two of us were surrounded by his herd of cattle, who were busy tucking into the soft, springy grass around the tent. I only got parts of what he was saying, but I didn't think he was too happy with where I'd pitched myself. I said that I'd be gone in an hour, to which he was satisfied, and he moved on. After a wash in the *çesme*, it was a beautifully tranquil morning once I was back on the road.

As pleasant as the scene was, I resented being stuck, once more, on a highway. Although it would be the last day for a while, I quickly missed the blissful silence of the hills in which I'd spent the night. The road was mostly deserted, less the odd gang of workers spreading fresh tarmac in the sun. Either side of the highway, kilometres of empty canvass stretched out, up to the feet of hills which stood as the only demarcation of space.

Having left Afyon, it was my intent to get through the town of Şuhut by the afternoon, and aim for one of the tiny villages on the other side to stay in for the evening. For whatever reason, it became clear at the outskirts of

Şuhut that I had quite badly run out of time for the day. As frustrating as it was, I re-planned to give myself a shorter day, and to be more disciplined the following morning. I also knew that after Şuhut, I wouldn't see another town for the rest of the leg, and I was keen to take advantage of it whilst I was here. *Better to rest, and ease myself back into the regimen of life on the road,* I reasoned with myself, trying to forgive him.

Passing a school, I realised I had arrived in time for Friday afternoon's rendition of the national anthem. A few parents and school kids spoke to me as I left. As I'd seen before, those more confident in their English relished the chance to practice 'good-bye!', as loudly as they could. It was always endearing. I found a cheap hotel in the centre of town. The room was hurriedly given a final clean by several men as I stood outside, which did little to clear the flies lazily circling below the ceiling.

Şuhut was a friendly small town, that seemingly wasn't doing too badly. Produce and workers from the surrounding countryside came and went on the same distinctive primitive trucks, filling the air with their distinctive *phat-phat* sound. I got some shirts washed, stocked up on some food for the next week, and had a simple dinner of *köfte*. The 'where are you from' spiel was, by this point, getting good. Or so I thought.

Day 37: *'Phat-Phat'*

Otel, Şuhut – Çeşme near Çobankaya
6th Nov 2021

Day 37's breakfast was in a pleasant little restaurant, full of families with children everywhere. The friendly owner sent his son over to me as many times as he could justify, to make sure I fully appreciated his English language skills. I got two meals, to make up for my poor diet the preceding few days, and to set me up for a long day.

I was sad to leave Şuhut. It had something of a historic character, which would have been nice to explore further, had I been afforded more time. As I joined the road heading south and out of town again, it wasn't long before the taxis and normal cars died off, and I was left with only tractors, trucks, and the endless rattle of those strange home-made vehicles. Having googled them, I discovered they were known as *phat-phats*.

I read later that they were developed by a man in Afyon municipality, who began building vehicles around a commonly-used water pump (which ran on cruder, cheaper fuel than diesel), and began selling them on. The basic model was little more than a chassis, an engine block and a wheel, sticking up from the driver's feet. Some had added bodywork to the front around the engine, with crude lights, a passenger seat, or just a bar to hold the driver back from falling in front of the wheels. Others had built full cabs around the steering wheel, side panels to keep produce in, or even a complete bodywork with canvas pulled tight over the back, to make a makeshift truck. Others were little more than four wheels and a steering bar, with produce or goods lashed onto the flat metal behind. In my experience, ownership of *phat-phats* was geographically restricted to the Afyon municipality, although I was told later that some had been exported as far as Afghanistan. I couldn't help but develop a strong admiration for the ingenuity and resourcefulness of their owners.

Regardless, any vehicles on the narrow country road outside of Şuhut would routinely pause on the road, to let shepherds heard their goats into freshly harvested fields. A group of women sat preparing crops that others had harvested that morning, tossing what looked like corn husks into the back of a few *phat-phats*. They waved me over, and offered me some bread and cheese for lunch after a short conversation. I got the feeling they didn't want to be disturbed in their work, so I settled down in the shade a few hundred metres later, and tore off chunks of cheese with the fresh bread.

As rural as it was, the south of Şuhut felt far more alive

than most of the empty wilderness I'd passed through. The main road for the day was long, straight, and mostly uneventful, stretching up to the hills of the next watershed. Around halfway across, a lone cattle herder beckoned me over to where he sat, in the shade of a few trees aside his cattle. He offered tea from a blackened pot resting on a few glowing coals. When I gladly accepted, he produced a second glass from an ornate wooden case. *Çay* was, after all, a sociable activity. We sat and chatted, watching the few white clouds drift by in the brightness of the early afternoon. We were only periodically interrupted by his cattle trying to stray into the road. Every five minutes or so, he would have to get up again, and persuade them back onto the vividly green grass with a few strikes of his staff.

Several kilometres later, I stopped in a tiny village, which had what seemed to be an improvised underpass, dug under the road for schoolchildren to cross safely. I paused to drink at the *çesme*, as I was now making a habit of doing: it was better to drink as you moved, than to deplete the water I was carrying, lest I run dry when I need some. This fountain was beautifully polished, with a stainless metal cup hanging from a chain to drink from. A kind old man informed me that the water came *"from in the mountains"*, and demonstrated that it was clean enough to drink straight from the pipe by cupping his hands and throwing the water over his face. I took the opportunity to ask about the *phat-phats*, what he did for work, and what to expect over the next week between here and Eğirdir. Curious, I asked about the prayer beads that he was carrying, passing slowly through his fingers as we spoke, similar to the way I had seen Roman Catholics do. Without a second's thought, he handed them to me, and refused profusely when I tried to offer them back to him. I protested, but he simply smiled when I tried to offer him some form of compensation. I would look after them well.

I finished the day's journey on an incline, winding up into the hills that separated Afyon's watershed from the next stage of the journey. I had planned to land in a small village just off from the main road. However, as the evening drew in, I came across a small *mescit*[17] with its own *çesme*, and resolved to spend the night there instead. I got the tent down in a small patch of soft grass, out of the view of the road. As the evening wound down, a feeling of peace settled as the frequency of lorries dwindled. Families would come and make stops next the *mescit*, before carrying on down the road to wherever their long journeys would take them. The sun setting,

---

[17] An Islamic place of prayer, smaller than a full mosque, similar to a Christian chapel.

being so far from any settlement made the idea of a fire quite appealing again. Trying to find enough material on the roadside, however, was a tough ask. The hedgerows and grounds were stripped bare, the only dry wood well out of reach. I eventually scraped together enough sticks and discarded roadside cardboard to get a small, enclosed campfire going.

As dusk approached, the familiar sounds of bells and hooves drifted over the gentle fields, and the evening's flock of sheep turned up. The shepherd, after skillfully guiding his flock across the road to drink, doubled back to come and speak to me. Looking at my meagre but workable attempt at a fire, he gave a broad, gaping smile. In an instant, he had dismounted his tiny donkey, had climbed one of the old ash trees I was camped under, and began vigorously shaking the dry branches and stripping huge chunks of dead bark from the tree. I was a little annoyed I hadn't thought of doing so myself, and could only stand at the bottom thinking of more ways to say 'thank you', as my new friend threw down great hunks of fuel for the fire.

With a now roaring fire and fuel aplenty, I enjoyed my evening meal of doner meat and bread. Content, I chose to sit outside to eat, and watched the last traces of the evening's sun disappear below the distant hills, which I'd been camped in only two days ago. As darkness fell, the horizon slowly began to glitter, as the residents of Şuhut switched on their lights for the evening. The stream of lorries carrying quarried marble northwards had finished for the day, and I was left alone with nothing but the gentle trickling of water from the *çeşme* to listen to. Although I was a little behind schedule, I could tolerate a day or more of life on the road, if only each evening could be as serene and settled as the one after Şuhut.

Day 38: 'Dust bowls and jackals'

Çeşme near Çobankaya – Roadside near Karacaören
7th Nov 2021

Determined to avoid the idleness of the last few mornings, as soon as dawn broke, I wasted no time in getting the fire re-kindled. Wanting to make the most of the fuel, I had a full, warm water wash prior to setting off. Enjoying the feeling of being clean, I bade farewell to the distant skyline of Şuhut.

The twenty kilometres that followed were nearly entirely empty. I crossed through two main watersheds, punctuated by the odd tiny village, but spoke to barely a soul. Empty fields covered the landscape in a patchwork of khaki brown, crisscrossed by tracks and low stone walls, only ending at the grey stone feet of the hills that divided each watershed. The tiny village of Uzunpınar was one of the only stops I made. It sat nestled beneath one of the hills, next to a broad plain inhabited yet again only by a herd of sheep. After midday, I rounded the base of another, and reached the second watershed that I had planned to cross that day. Coming off the road, I followed a lone track through the fields, leaving behind everything for eight kilometres.

Seeing the terrain that I had to cover laid bare, with so

little around and so little cover, was somehow intimidating. The hills around the basin felt as though they were watching me, forebodingly, as I trespassed into a space which was so thoroughly empty. I was the only human as far as the eye could see in any direction, which felt uncanny in the same way one would feel walking onto a sports pitch in front of a crowd. The emptiness held a somewhat foreboding aura. As I made slow progress, however, that feeling developed into a sense of tangible achievement. The day's progress was not best seen on a map, or measured in hours or kilometres. I could measure it in features on the horizon, or distant landmarks that faded into the haze of the afternoon. Foreboding turned into a sense of accomplishment, marked out in real time.

It was hot work, and walking due south involved walking right into the sun for most of the day. The fine dust in the centre of the track coated my boots and trousers, and was impossible to shake off. The basin was intersected by a road crossing east to west, about two kilometres from the southern hills. On it stood a petrol station, and to my delight, an open restaurant. I gorged on sausage and fried eggs, grateful for some freshly prepared protein. As I enjoyed the fresh air around my feet, listened to the sparrows in the roof, and chatted with a stranger about their recommendations in acoustic Turkish music, time raced on without me. The sun began to dip, and I realised I still had a lot of ground to cover. I was once again racing the daylight.

The original plan for the evening was to reach a small village called Karacaören, as there was no chance of me crossing the steep hills that preceded Lake Eğirdir until the next day. Had I started an hour or so earlier that morning, I could have made it, but at around 17:30 I began to up the pace, watching the light start to fade. A lovely couple passed me in a tractor, the wife sitting on a pile of fruit in their trailer, and they offered me a lift. I was sorely tempted to take it, but not having a certain way to get dropped back to where I had got to, I insisted on walking. They offered me their house number and a place to camp in the village (something about a football pitch), should I get there. As darkness fell, I realised that my efforts wouldn't cut it. It would be another night in a bush somewhere.

Finding a gap in the rows upon rows of fruit trees either side of the road, I tacked right into the orchards. Getting into the shrubland at the foot of the hill was difficult going, as deep ditches left by ploughing had dried into mounds, which were lethal to the unsuspecting ankle. Darkness continued to set in, with still no flat ground to be found. I began to run, dipping past low hanging branches and tripping on stones and clods of dirt. I tripped once, and fell into the sharp, baked dry earth. In frustration, I dropped the pack, and continued to scour the ground for anywhere flat, and receptive to a tent.

Eventually finding a patch of long, springy grass next to a cluster of trees, I rushed to clear a space to pitch on. I'd have been more relaxed, were it not for the combination of the lack of permission, the lack of potential help, and the lack of time to get a shelter together. The sound of engines a few fields over, and the occasional splash of brightness from a headlight, was my main worry as I zipped the tent shut.

It wouldn't stay that way. I would come to regret not making better progress into the village a few hours before morning. At around 03:00, I was awoken by the screeches and howls of multiple packs of creatures. There were at least two groups of several each, one group very much closer than the other. I recorded the screeching and howls, and after some deliberation, some friends and I concluded that I'd been kept up by two packs of jackals. It was most inconsiderate of them.

Day 39: 'Squatting done right'

Day 39 began with an acute water shortage. Having simply dropped myself in the middle of nowhere, I was reliant on only what I had carried with me. Fortunately, Karacaören had a *çesme* and a well-stocked *bakkal*, which afforded all the opportunity I needed to restock.

Despite this, I didn't feel particularly welcome. The shopkeeper seemed to eye me with a measure of suspicion, as I brought a few loaves of bread and cheese, as did the group of men sat enjoying coffee in the mid-morning sun opposite. When I tried to ask for directions up into the hills, I was directed downhill. When I tried to explain that no, the map said there was a direct path this way, I was ushered back. Not wishing to cause a scene, and probably not knowing enough words to argue my side anyway, I left. On my way out of the village, I passed the football pitch that the couple had mentioned the night before. Seeing it covered in burnt rubbish piles, shards of glass and twisted metal, I counted myself lucky not to have tried pitching a tent at night there. I enjoyed lunch on a secluded viewing spot, looking back over the last few days, before starting up the final hills towards Lake Eğirdir.

A short, winding road took the occasional passing vehicle through the hills towards the lake. It crossed a few dramatic little valleys, meandering through the peaks, avoiding the highest points along the way. It was still something of a shock to the system to transition to hills as quickly as the geography demanded, but not hugely taxing. Slaloming around the road, swapping lanes to stay out of the paths of the occasional traffic, it didn't take long to break through to the other side. It took a second for the view to register.

I became physically emotional only twice between Kefken and Antalya. Both times did not, as I might have predicted prior to setting off, come from feelings of physical pain, anger, or frustration. In the same way that I had welled up for the first time, looking back over at Geyve on my way towards Eskişehir, I could not have foreseen how moving the sight of sheer landscapes would be. Looking out onto Lake Eğirdir was the second such moment. The mountains from whence I'd come rolled down into a vast expansive valley, interwoven by canals and treelines, snaking around a tributary into the lake. Dead ahead, at least two days walk in the distance, the peaks of Mount Barla stood forebodingly over the whole scene. In the far distance, a thin sliver of water glistened in the sunlight, surrounding the base of the mountain. On that lake, I knew, sat the end of this stage, and a proper bed. Both then, and back past Geyve, the emotional high of the situation felt enhanced, enormously, by a sense of isolation. I imagined that very few Britons had seen the same view, from the same vantage point, that I had. Fewer still would have spent the days and weeks prior sleeping in the dirt on the roadside to get there. The hard times were occasionally rewarding in their own right, but the good times were always made more powerful for the sweat it took to reach them.

Having let the emotional high subside, I began walking down the meandering road towards the floor of the wide valley. Walking downhill was, again, my worst enemy. My feet felt shoved into the front of my boots, cramping my toes, and pressing on those areas which had become delicate after miles of trudging. My knees and joints felt every jolt, as I continually fought to stop the momentum from carrying me away, and carrying me downhill. There was no way of mitigating it. Whereas the exhaustion of inclines comes and goes, walking downhill is a constant drain. I rolled around the hairpin bends ever downwards, with each step the glistening water of the lake getting slightly closer.

I paused at the foot of the hills to get my bearings. I was through with most of the day's descent, but the question of where to land for the evening remained. Five *dolmuş* taxis passed, in a loose convoy. I waved, and got five vehicle horns in response. It was a small victory, which I felt more than proportionately in that moment. I returned to trying to deal with a new blister that had formed deep between two toes. Unable to reach it, but unable to put up with the swelling any longer, I dug a sanitised needle further into my foot, desperate to relieve some of the pressure, and hit a nerve. With a jolt I cried out, feeling as though I might vomit there and then, on the side of the road. Unsuccessful, another layer of tape was applied.

My original plan had been to cross the valley at the perpendicular, resting for the evening near one of the villages on the far side, at the base of the mountain. True to form, I had massively overestimated how far I could get in a day, and was again faced with the question of where to make camp. Covered in orchards, and crossed by deep thick furrows from ploughing, there was little flat ground to take, let alone any concealed from view or obviously available. Crossing the valley, I darted into the low fruit trees occasionally, looking for anywhere which could accommodate a tent for the night, without success. Finally, as dusk approached, I came across a patch of spare land, littered with abandoned concrete pipe sections and construction site debris. I threw the tent down behind a pile of concrete scraps, largely obscured from the road by the debris.

For whatever reason, I felt sullen as I strolled over to the nearby petrol station, after darkness had fallen. I was resistant to the understandably curious questioning of the attendants, after buying a few bottles of water and some food. Had I continued the conversation, I'm sure he would have recommended moving the tent closer to his house, or even offered somewhere to stay, but I had no energy left to do so. I thanked him and left, walking back into the deep blackness. Whereas the night before, I had kept a low profile to try and avoid attention from whatever nocturnal creatures lurked, I opted for a different strategy. Sticking a light on, and singing softly to myself, I dared anything in the bushes to come and find me. I was past caring.

Day 40: 'Welcome to the Med'

Roadside near Gençali – Roadside near Bagcagız
9ᵗʰ Nov 2021

Watching the sun rise over the lake was a brief moment of escapism from the dirty, off-grid squatting I found myself engaged in. It was a highly introverted experience, and more-so than other parts, had felt very much 'in the dirt'. As pre-arranged back in Eskişehir, I tried to call the Fairbairn brothers, sat on a lump of concrete as my stove brought some water up to the boil. There was no answer. I'd try again some other time.

I had made the most of the piercing morning's sunrise by charging the two phones and battery pack as I broke camp. Doing so was becoming a larger part of the routine, as I spent more time away from people and 'off the grid'. As I went back to pick up the devices, I found the lot covered in a thick carpet of black ants. They had, for whatever reason, made themselves at home in every nook and cranny of the solar panel, phones, battery pack and assorted cables, and it took a great deal of brushing down and shaking to get them out. With some spare *kolonya*, I tried to see how many I could set alight. It proved tougher than expected.

I returned to the same petrol station to get some more

water and other supplies. The owner was impressed to hear that I'd come all the way from the coastline that was, now, the further one away. Having stocked up on water, I set out into the cool morning air again, to reach the far side of the valley, and as far onwards as possible.

One single road ran perpendicular to the course of the river, parallel to the lake, coming to an end at the foot of the next mountain. It stretched unbending across the vast expanse I had to cover for the day, which only seemed to get larger as the day wore on. The constant canopy of fruit trees stretched as far as could be seen, forming a patchwork carpet of browns and greens. It was punctuated by great piles of apples and plums, piled up by diggers, and driven out by lorry. The strong scent of fruit, a little sickly in the sun, lingered.

Eventually, I crossed the main riverbed. Checking the route, I found that I was able to cut off a few kilometres by walking straight over the dried-up river delta, which stretched intimidatingly wide off to my left. I left the road, and began crossing. My only company was a flock of sheep, driven by a shepherd hundreds of metres away. He was too far off to greet, so we exchanged a lingering, confused silence instead. A *kangal* limped on behind them, before approaching me. I tried to offer some water to the poor animal, to no avail, and had to leave it hobbling after it's herd and master. I had the distinctly unpleasant sensation of seriously needing to relieve myself, but still hundreds of metres away from any bush or tree, I had to limp on.

Finally hitting the main road to Eğirdir, the distinguishably lived-in villages felt eerily quiet. Eventually, I entered the second village, Akkeçili, desperate for some form of food by the afternoon. I bumped into a lad around my age, who very kindly offered me some unleavened bread and tomatoes, which I warmly accepted. I ate the thin, grainy husks in the shade of a small orchard, in the thin strip of land between mountain and lake, in which the settlements resided. Potentially, it was the sight of olive trees, or even just the sound of gentle waves on the lake's shoreline below. Possibly, it was just nice to be in the sun but out of the wind. Whichever it was, the atmosphere upon meeting the lake felt definitively Mediterranean. That in turn, felt like progress, somehow. Following the twists and turns of the shoreline road, I came across a secluded camping spot, probably used by groups when in-season. It would have made the perfect place to spend the night, had I had access to water. I tried to reach the edge of the lake but found it impossible. A crisp white layer of crusted lake silt disguised the thick mud beneath, putting any immediate access to the lake out of reach. Faced with the dilemma of where to go, I consulted Maps, and found a few patches of green next to the lake a few kilometres on. Once more, I was chasing the landscape for a quiet patch of grass, and was being chased by the coming night.

After a few false starts and a few kilometres of pacing it out, a suitable spot appeared. A rolling grassy verge led down to a rock-strewn beach, where the thick reeds lining the shoreline gave way to clear, gentle water. Not only did I now have water to drink, but the prospect of a proper wash beckoned, temptingly. I left that for the next morning.

As evening rolled in, I was worried that my proximity to the lake's edge would place me on a route used by animals to drink, and built another fire. I spent far too long trying to rip branches from trees and scrounge firewood on the side of the road, and far too little time getting food together. When I did, having lost the light, the result was a disaster. My attempts to mix some tomatoes from earlier with pasta I was carrying fell wholly flat, leaving me bitingly hungry, and with a lot of washing up for the morning. I launched the failed, soggy lump of starch as far away from the tent as I could throw, and left the pot for the next morning. I slept, starving.

Day 41: *"Çay, gel!"*

Keen to seize the pristine morning, it felt only right to try and get an early morning swim in. Stripping off in the brisk breeze, in the hope that no passing cars would spot my secluded corner, I waded gingerly into the lake, not entirely sure what awaited my feet below the surface. I managed a few minutes afloat, letting the clear, cold waves carry off layers of sweat and dirt. As bracing as the waters were, the feeling of being clean again was always something I looked forward to. Ice baths are supposedly meant to be good for you, anyway.

Being cold and soaked through always makes you truly appreciate being warm and dry. With fleece layers back on, I rekindled the fire, and enjoyed breakfast and a few coffees as the sun began to pick up over the lake. The mist hanging over the water was slowly burned off, as the sun climbed higher into a spotless sky. It was one of the most serene moments of the trip. I felt blessed to hold that space, having panicked the evening before that I might be left without somewhere. My own little corner of the world lay perfectly idyllic, as I watched the ripples of the lake shimmer in the morning's glow, undisturbed by anything. I was at peace.

It was at that point that a huge *kangal* dog appeared from behind a tree. Clocking me, it crept forward, flopped over, and expectantly looked up, waiting for attention. The dog's owner followed thereafter. Hasan was a shepherd, whose thick beard and sideburns met a crumpled woolen hat, encircling his face. He was a jolly character, who wasted no time in telling me about his sons who worked in Isparta and the surrounding villages. Hasan's flock of sheep trudged after him in search of greenery. He held a polished, curved shepherd's cane, and he used it to bend pine branches down for his flock to nibble on. I realised, as his sheep filled the little corner to gorge on branches and tufts of grass, that I was probably camped on one of his routine bits of grazing land. Hasan assured me there was no rush, but I felt imposing, so began throwing the contents of the tent into my pack with as much speed as I could muster. I could re-pack properly later. Hasan gave me a number for a heavily worn-down Nokia 3310, should I ever need it, and we departed with much jovial handshaking. I jumped the crash barrier, and was back on the road.

The rest of the day passed slowly, more or less without event. The road undulated a fair amount, despite running next to a lake, and I was on constant lookout for closely passing trucks. Huge articulated lorries would come speeding around the narrow corners, not leaving much room across the two lanes for anything else. Although the morning's strong breeze kept the day cool, the bright blue of the lake and dazzling sunlight maintained the feeling of being somewhere profoundly more Mediterranean. Despite passing through numerous villages, I saw barely a soul.

My destination for the day was Barla, a village a couple of kilometres up into the hills from the lakeside. It promised, apparently, a few hotels and hostels, as well as some shops from which to restock. Having trudged up the steep hillside into the first outskirts of the place, I called over to a man working, to ask about places to stay. He denied that there were any. I was confused, and pushed on up the hills further. Sure enough, all three places listed were well and truly closed for the winter. In hindsight, I would have been lucky to find somewhere open in such a remote location. In the moment, however, I was just bitterly disappointed. I'd worked my hopes up for something that was, realistically, unrealistic. I was now cold, quite tired, and a few kilometres off the plan.

The owner of a tiny corner shop helped turn the afternoon around. He invited me to join him and his two colleagues for çay, and I recounted a few stories of the journey thus far as I warmed up around their stove. After buying my fill of food, he suggested I make camp in the village's park immediately behind his shop. I was very grateful, being entirely stuck for other places to go. Pitching in the wind was a pain, but not impossible. I settled down, happy enough that this would be my last night in a tent before Eğirdir, and began to tuck into some bread and cheese.

It was then that a voice called out. On its second try, I realised the owner was talking to me, and I got out of the tent (a difficult task to do with any dignity with someone standing over you). Two individuals had pitched up. One was a loud, young-ish man, who insisted repeatedly that there was a hostel nearby that I was invited to stay at, with *çay* (emphasised). The other appeared to be his child, whose name entirely failed to help me work out which gender they could possibly be.

There then followed a very difficult conversation, which shoved the limits of my ability to speak as far as they could go. The two were insistent that I follow them, and that I get a lift to some place. I explained that, although it was very kind of them to offer, I was completely happy where I was. They warned that I would be too cold. I countered with a fumbled attempt at explaining I was used to it. They warned I would get in trouble with the police. Way out in the sticks, I didn't buy this for a second, and I explained that the shop owner had given me permission. They re-explained their offer (with *çay*, again, emphasised), and I explained that it would take too long to pack down, that I had a lot of stuff, and I was very tired and wanted to go to sleep. My explanation being lacking, they would start again. We repeated the process a few times over. Energy levels entirely depleted, I was insistent that, come what may, I would not be moving.

To get out of the bizarre semi-confrontation, I agreed to share a glass of tea or two with them over in a nearby hut. I was introduced to a host of villagers, each of whom had a real name and an assigned nickname of some sort. Tragically, I can't recall any, but they were given out according to their jobs within the village, I think. They told me that they'd grow fruit in the hills, and fish from the lake whilst the hotels was out of season, as a way of making ends meet. As the hut filled up with more villagers through the evening, everyone around was warm and welcoming. The two characters from earlier were understanding when I had my last *çay*, and walked back out into the thick black night. One more night to Eğirdir.

Day 42: 'A dog called Boris'

Park, Barla – Charly's Pansiyon, Eğirdir
11ᵗʰ Nov 2021

The morning was, once more, beautifully bright, and bitingly cold. After a quick glass of *çay* with the corner shop owner, as I resumed the job of breaking camp, the man who'd offered *çay* the night before tried again. Wanting nothing more than to be making progress by now, I tried to explain *"I have already had some"* but evidently failed, as his request was repeated another three times. He eventually gave up. I felt a little awkward, but threw the pack on, and began walking.

I was dazzled by the sunlight as I wandered back down towards the lakeside road. A metallic silhouette of a police car greeted me. They were fairly common on the roads, even coming with their own flashing lights for effect, but seemed to have little effect on the traffic flying past. I stopped to cross the road, pausing for a second, when a dog wandered up.

I was confused, certain for a while that he had an owner. He was a retriever-like breed, with reasonably well-kept, thick blonde fur. He seemed to savour the chance to look photogenic, as I snapped away against the backdrop of the lake. Quite fancying some company for the coming day at this point, I offered him a couple of biscuits, and he was sold. The day's companion had been acquired. Sure enough, the rest of the day was a monotonous slog, combining the unpleasant walking surface of constant asphalt with the twists, turns and climbs of a country lane.

Unfortunately, the concept of walking by the road, as opposed to in the centre of the road, never quite clicked for my new friend. I would walk in the oncoming lane, as usual, with the dog behind me. He would then, like clockwork, pad round to my right-hand side, staying level with me for a minute, before getting bored and wandering into the middle of the road. Much shouting and shoving with a stick failed to solve this, and I resigned myself to his potential fate. Nothing would deter him from owning both lanes, and quickly, the number of angry truck drivers and motorcyclists grew. As they veered around the dog, they would regularly raise a hand at me, one even coming to a halt to yell words to the effect of *"what the hell are you doing?"*. I could only reply with *"I don't know him"*, several times over, pointing stupidly at the lump of fur sprawled over the asphalt. Blonde, independent-minded, a lover of photo ops but thoroughly stupid, he bore an uncanny similarity to the British Prime Minster at the time. I christened him 'Boris'.

Boris and I shared some bread for lunch outside the

world's tiniest mosque, next to a waterfront property somewhere between two villages. The mosque's minaret was composed of a few oil drums stacked atop each other, which was a level of creativity I deeply appreciated. A few kilometres down the road, I came across a small wood, with access to a stony beach on the lakeside. I sat back on the pack, and took some time to reflect. It was the 11th of November, and 14:00 in Turkey coincided with the national moment of remembrance back in Britain. It was the first time I can remember honouring the fallen in quite such an isolated way. Yet, standing on the lake's shore, with only the gentle rustling of foliage to distract, I felt intimately connected to those back in the UK doing likewise.

The only other person on the road that day was another goat herder, who was making best use of the bushes on the steep hillside to my right to feed his flock on. Like me, not getting hit by passing traffic was his main worry, as he forcefully shoved his animals back into the gutter when they wandered astray. We exchanged a glance, and nothing more.

The final approach to Eğirdir was another long, unpleasant final stretch. Although 22 kilometres was not an unreasonable target, the constant tarmac surface left my feet loudly complaining towards the last eight. I fought off the urge to pause where I was and jump back into the lake, even for a few minutes. Boredom found a way of exacerbating the physical pain and mental frustration, and the lack of variance in the seemingly endless road had its own way of reminding you that there was no way out but on.

Aside from a hefty number of tourists, Eğirdir is also home to the Turkish Army's commando training facility, the mountainous terrain and lake offering abundant training opportunities for the specialised troops. Coming up on the last peninsula before the town, I spotted a column of commandos on exercise. Carrying full kit, sleeping mats and rifles, a well-spaced patrol snaked its way off the lake's edge, ran parallel to my road, and then crossed up ahead before diving up into the mountains. As I got closer, they clocked me. I politely offered a greeting as I walked through the patrol. I walked on a few paces, before a soldier, presumably a junior leader, called out to me. Jokingly, he raised his rifle for a second, before lowering it, smiling, and asking where I was from. We conversed briefly.

Not overly keen to be near someone with a visibly loaded weapon for too long, I tried to move off, but Boris had busied himself making friends with another soldier, who was trying to oversee the road crossing fifty metres away.

Angrily ordered, I think, to control the dog, I tried to explain myself. Failing, I just started walking, ignoring the troops, hoping Boris would follow as I got far enough away. Fortunately, he did.

Even as Eğirdir came into view, the road veered up and down through the final hills, as if trying for one last time to throw me off before I could finally rest. Eğirdir is a single peninsula, from which a tiny, seaside-esque town spills onto the lakeside, hugging the feet of Mount Sivri. I had decided on a plan to leave Boris with some food, seeing as he'd covered nearly 20 kilometres with me, and let him roam the outskirts of the town. Before I could do so, however, he had already run off into the town, leaving me stood with a packet of cheap sausages I'd brought for his efforts. As stressful as his presence was, I hope he ended up somewhere pleasant, which didn't involve walking.

My last push through the town took me past the commando barracks, and into town. The bitter wind, deserted, stony beaches, and tired-looking hotels could have been anywhere on the coast of England. As darkness fell, it felt steadily more surreal to be in a populated area again. On other days, the transition from rural to urban had happened over the course of a day. In Eğirdir, I felt as though I had dived back into populated, bustling, 'normal' life within minutes. A few passers-by stopped and commented on my appearance. I didn't stop to listen.

I hadn't rung ahead to test if the guesthouse (*pansiyon*) was open, given that Eğirdir was far larger than Barla. The *pansiyon* was a short walk out onto the peninsula. Struggling to stay on my feet by now, I wondered what I'd do or where I'd go if it wasn't open. Trudging back down the peninsula, into the blackness, was too ugly a prospect to even consider. Finding the place, I knocked on a thick metallic door, and a tall, dark-haired man opened it.

"*Charly's pansiyon' mi?*" "*Evet.*"

"*Bos oda var mı?*" "*Evet.*"

"*İngilizce konuşuyor musun?*" "*Evet.*"

The rest of the evening was something of a blur. Matt Krause and I had literally, finally, crossed paths.

Days 43 – 48: 'Just one more day'

Resting in Eğirdir
12th Nov – 16th Nov 2021

In his own book, Matt Krause described just how seductive a place Eğirdir could be. He stayed longer than he originally intended, detailing how hard it was to actually leave, and carry on his journey from the Aegean to the Iranian border. Very quickly, I understood what he meant. The *pansiyon* was a collection of buildings, including a few houses of rooms, and a central building with views overlooking all of the tiny town and the lake, where I ate well. The town felt sleepier during the day, as a slow trickle of tourists filtered through.

The place was owned by the man I had met the night before, İbrahim. He employed an English woman, Carla, who came to stay for a few months each year. Along with two girls who were working whilst travelling, Marie from France and Anna from Russia, and a local lad called Jihad, I had plenty of company. Other travellers passed through continuously, despite the season, and I found friends from the US, Belgium, France, Jordan and Scotland. I was the youngest of the various nomads and couples who drifted by, but I didn't mind. The change from being largely isolated, chilly, and hungry, was very welcome. I even managed to see a friend from Eskişehir, who came down to visit the serene, secluded corner of the country.

I managed a second lake swim one morning before breakfast. Having had my fill of feeling brittle, and tasting the occasional hint of lake weed and goose faeces, I didn't return. The extent of my exploring was sadly limited to a short boat trip around the lake. I would have loved to have seen more, and to have joined my new-found pals on a trip up Mount Sivri, but the thought of climbing up another mountain was too much to comprehend. Instead, I spent the time updating the journal, attempting (as ever) to refresh my grasp of the language, buying some warmer clothing, and enjoying a few late evenings.

Whilst there, finally, I managed to arrange a fleeting phone conversation with the Fairbairn brothers for one of their podcast episodes. I dreaded to think how my own voice sounded, uploaded onto Spotify for all to hear, yet eagerly anticipated the episode's arrival. It was a strange turn of events that had played out, but I was grateful for a lighter, more entertaining side to the trip that my interactions with them had brought. I eagerly awaited the episode's release.

The remaining time I had was spent pensively wandering the peninsula. Once the wind calmed down, the entire lake took on a millpond-esque tranquillity. A thick layer of fog would often cover the horizon, so that identifying where mirror-like lake ended and sky began became all but impossible. The only break on the seamless surface would be the occasional fishing boat, each ripple of the wake casting a long shadow. Once, the peninsula had been home to Greek-speaking monastic communities, who no doubt would have spent much of their time in contemplative silence. In those serene shoreside moments, I understood why.

It was here that the idea of changing Stage 4 was first suggested to me. My original plan was just to crack on with the route suggested by Maps. It was the quickest path to the sea, and at this stage, that was all I wanted to get to. However, sat as I was in a very beautiful setting, and recalling the weeks of toil I'd spent on asphalt until now, I never wanted to see another highway again. So, when İbrahim and Carla suggested I take another route, I was all ears.

There was a trail from Eğirdir through to Antalya, known as the St Paul's Way. I had first heard about the Way prior to planning the whole journey, months before. It would take me away from the highways, and up into the enormously remote hills and valleys north of Antalya, at one stage leading along a canyon through a national park. It was an additional day's walk at least, and a good few hundred metres more of hills. Yet, the last time I took a more rural detour back in Stage Two, as difficult as the Çukurca day ended up being, the whole experience was richly rewarding. Feeling adventurous, I spent a day on the sunlit top floor of the *pansiyon*, poring over maps, apps and guidebooks, trying to plan.

No single (reliable) guide to the route existed. However, I was advised that there were similar *pansiyons*, shops, amenities and understanding locals along the route, accustomed to walkers. I was also advised that it was not only a well-trodden path, but a clearly signposted one, too.

It should be easy, then, I thought.

53: My own personal highway, north of Belkaracaören.

54: Donkey-born shepherds drive their flocks homewards for the night, Belkaracaören.

240

55: A fire provides some reassurance, Belkaracaören.

56: Enjoying tea whilst the cattle herder keeps his flock away from the road, south of Şuhut.

57: The mescit and çeşme near Çobankaya, my small roadside sanctuary for the evening.

58: Pausing for water, en route to Karacaören.

59: Mid-stride.

60: My first glimpse of Lake Eğirdir.

61: Tranquillity, aside Lake Eğirdir.

62: Hasan and flock.

63: The Lake itself. In the far-left corner, the final turn before the peninsula came into view can be seen.

64: Barla Mosque, early morning.

65: A brief moment of remembrance, on the trot.

66: Boris. Unusually, pictured here on the edge of the road, rather than straight into oncoming traffic.

67A, 67B & 67C: Boris makes a friend - a story in three parts.

68: Eğirdir, from Charly's pansiyon.

69A & 69B: Once the driving southerly winds had died down, Eğirdir took on a magical sense of stillness.

Leg Four

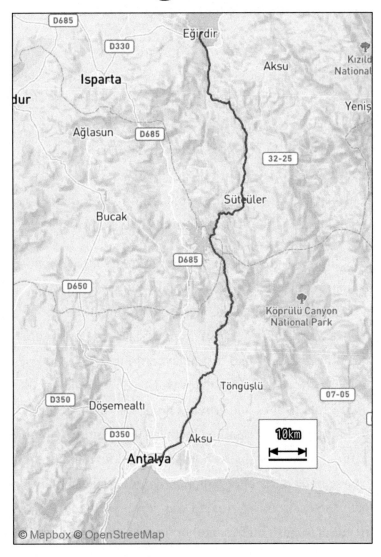

Eğirdir (Isparta) –Antalya

Day 49: 'Three beers!'

Charly's Pansiyon, Eğirdir – Serpil (Charly's Pansiyon, Eğirdir)
17ᵗʰ Nov 2021

My original plan had been to stay for three nights. A week later, one mildly hungover morning, I began moving again. There would be few places to stay around where I planned to finish that first day, so I planned to hitchhike back to the *pansiyon* for one (finally final) night, before returning the next day to where I left off. After that, Stage 4 would begin fully. The next stop would be Antalya.

Despite the protests of İbrahim and Carla, I insisted on taking all of the kit with me, despite knowing I'd be coming back to spend the night there again. It felt wrong to give myself a lighter load, as practical and sensible as it might have been. I had carried everything so far, and I would carry it the rest of the way. Not only would it feel like cheating, but I had grown a grudging fondness for the feeling of freedom signified by living like a turtle, with my entire home on my back. It was the freedom to, over the course of days, fly over hills and rivers, taking whichever path I so desired. Wherever I was, it represented the freedom to push on for another hour or so.

Turning off the road which followed the shoreline, to begin heading due south along a canal, was like flipping a switch. Instantly, I was back in the same rural-industrial orchards of the week before I arrived in Eğirdir. One dead-straight road bisected the valley for the rest of the day, with very little room for both the numerous lorries and I. Eventually, I was able to swap onto a dirt track running adjacent to the road and canal. Being off the tarmac and back on dirt was at least mildly comforting.

Yet, being surrounded by the same rows of trees and flat fields, and stuck on the unchanging, straight due-south path, made the going truly monotonous. A kilometre or so out in either direction lay the feet of great hills, rock formations, and the odd isolated village nestled on the high ground, commanding the landscape in either direction. Yet, up close and personal, all I had to contend with was orchards, truck parks, lorries, and the occasional patch of grazing ground. Monotony, as I knew by now, made everything harder. Having lazed around Eğirdir for a full week had hardly helped either. The process of getting back into walking, putting one foot in front of the other for hours on end until the sun got low enough that you could go home, wherever the hell that was, was disorienting. Out of boredom, I found myself checking the map often, to try and track my progress, wishing away the distance. I was met with disbelief each time.

Aside from having to ford the odd stream, which seemed

easier in the moment than re-routing for two kilometres, absolutely nothing worthy of note happened. As the sun began to dip off to my right, casting its lurid shadows across the valley, I reached my pre-ordained point where I would dive off into the hills, to go and find this trail. Over the road, a husband and wife struggled to get a dated red tractor out of a huge rut. I was about to offer a hand, before the wife's efforts pushed the machine onto firmer ground, and it pulled itself clear of the mud. She jumped onto the back of their trailer, and I waved the duo off as they sailed on their way.

The process of hitch-hiking back took longer than I planned for. I had been told many times that it'd be easy, and I had imagined the idea of flagging down a willing volunteer would be quite simple. Yet, as the minutes mounted up, and the sun only got lower, I began to think about a plan B. Admittedly, had I been driving, and seen the size and weight of this scraggy traveller's kit, I probably wouldn't have picked him up either. After about 20 minutes of standing about, waving my thumb around in vain, a van indicated right, and slowed. "*Eğirdir? Evet.*" The main pack in the back of the van, I squeezed into the front, sandwiched between the driver and his mate.

The driver was far more interested in talking to me than driving. Whilst I'm sure he was simply trying to be courteous, I'd much rather he had have kept his eyes on the road, than facing me. We mostly managed to stay in our lane. Getting going, the driver asked if I liked beer. I replied in the affirmative. He said something about *"three beers!"*, which I didn't understand. I eventually concluded that the half-empty can of *Efes* beer he was holding was, in all probability, his third beer of the evening.

Arriving back in Eğirdir, somewhat glad to have survived the journey, I stayed one final night at the *pansiyon* before moving off the next day. Once more, I had very little appetite to leave at all. The contrast of being back on the road once more, only to come back to sitting comfortably in front of a full plate of warm food, knowing that I'd be back on the road the next morning, was a jarring contrast. I slept soundly, enjoying my last night in a proper bed for some time.

Day 50: 'There should be a path here.'

Serpil – Field, Direskene
18ᵗʰ Nov 2021

I had one last familiar breakfast of bread, cheese, *hash-hash*[18] and honey, before bidding my final farewells to İbrahim, Carla, Marie, Anna, and Jihad. Wandering into town, I found a taxi, and managed to describe the rough area (at least the nearest village) to where I'm hoping he'll drop me. The drive back was an awful lot safer than the van journey the day before. A little bemused, the taxi dropped me back at the bridge near Serpil, and I crossed the tiny bridge over the canal, heading for the hills.

A hundred metres or so later, some workers at a vineyard called me over for tea, but I excused myself, needing to make progress. An attempt to cut across a field failed, which resulted in me doing an embarrassing U-turn in front of the aforementioned workers. As I walked past yet-more fruit fields, a man busy harvesting by hand gifted me a surprisingly large apple, despite my protests that I had no means to carry it. Two other workers also tried to offer things for the journey, but I had to decline. It was quite the welcome back into the countryside.

---

[18] A thick, doughy pastry, served alongside other breakfast items. Best eaten with honey. Despite contemporary English similarities, unrelated to cannabis.

Reaching the foot of the hills, a harsh sun had begun to beat down. A group of kids on bikes cycled past, and after hearing where I was headed, were keen for selfies all round.

It was at the foot of these hills near Serpil, that I would leave the roads and paths I had followed via Maps, and join the St Paul's Way. The best mapping I had for the Way was a different app, which wasn't wholly reliable. Roughly estimating where I was meant to be going, I began walking up what I assumed to be the path, which ran parallel to a dried-up riverbed, climbing into the hills. As the path meandered closer to the riverbed, before vanishing altogether, I should have realised that I had made quite a considerable error. There was no way it would be possible to traverse this route, not least when the river was actually running. Nevertheless, convinced each corner I rounded would offer a solution, I hoped that an obvious sign would present itself. Eventually meeting a solid wall of rock, under what would usually be a waterfall when the river would run, I had no choice but to think again.

I was already feeling a bit exhausted, and so dropped the pack and had some lunch, nestled in the shadow of a very large boulder. I reasoned that although I'd missed the path's entrance, the original route would run parallel to the riverbed, further up the steep valley edges. I therefore decided to try half scrambling, half climbing up the steep embankment, to see if it was possible to break out and find the original path. If I couldn't find it, I would have to turn back and try again tomorrow, putting me badly behind schedule.

And so, I began scrambling. It was hands and feet work, up and across the constantly sliding scree. Even knowing by now to avoid the smaller stones or gravel, and to stick to larger boulders, it was difficult going. I lost my footing on one occasion, sliding back a metre or so, but only dislodging a few smaller rocks in the process. Once I'd regained composure, I pressed on. After climbing up the side of a fallen tree, now lying down the hill, I reached what appeared to be an actual, workable path. Surely, this had to be it. I dropped back into the valley, remounted my pack, and stashed my walking sticks behind my shoulders. This would be the difficult bit.

The additional weight, and energy it would take to lift my stuff up out of the steep incline, was the least of my worries. With my centre of gravity so changed, the climb back up was tough to navigate safely. I felt far less nimble, and had to test each position more diligently to avoid slipping again. If I lost my footing, it would have been much harder to recover it. I was practically crawling uphill for much of the journey, hugging the dirt. Once more, the fallen tree was useful to climb up. However, as I reached the trunk's halfway point, I felt the whole log slip. I froze, before very gently moving back onto the scree, digging small holds for my hands and feet as I went. Once I dismounted, the tree was detached, and began sliding down the steep slope. As it picked up speed, I watched in something of a fascinated horror as the whole thing careened down the valley, gathering force and bringing smaller, then larger, rocks and debris with it. It landed on the valley's floor with a tremendous crash, and the patter of rocks smashing against the ground. I took a minute or so, and traversed over to the edges of my route up, to stay away from any other loose areas. After what felt like an age, I summited the valley.

Now with a firm path, I picked up the pace. I was sheltered by trees for the rest of the day's progress, and had largely soft moss or earth underfoot. As the path joined a vehicle track, I overtook cattle walking back to their village, in groups of two or three. Such was their routine, they had trodden their own path into the centre of the road, a darker trail of mud that wound around the tiny contours of the track. Each group would stop as I passed them, inquisitively, before resuming their walk home as I had passed.

I emerged out of a thick pine canopy just as the sun was beginning to dip below the horizon, into the small village of Direşkene. Two children playing with a puppy spotted me coming up the path, and nervously asked where I'd come from. Very politely, they asked if I needed anything, and I was duly offered plentiful water to refill from (and then tea, of course), by their father. In the course of throwing a frisbee for the two children, I accidentally managed to hit the puppy, but the whole family found this quite funny. A few other children pushed one of their friends along in a toy car, speeding around the corners of a real road without a care in the world.

Trying to find somewhere to land was a little more difficult. The first couple I spoke to suggested that there was nowhere suitable nearby, despite there being plenty of spaces of spare dirt around. Having found a corner of a patch of grass, some bloke leant out of a window to ask what I'm up to, giving the standard upturned palm gesture to ask *"why"*? He introduced himself as Mustafa, and once I asked if I could camp next to his house, he agreed. Hoping that I wasn't turfing out any cows from their usual grazing spot (again) I shoved the tent as far into a corner as I could for some privacy, and nipped up to the nearest mosque to collect water. It was another unforgivingly freezing night.

Day 51: 'Swings & roundabouts'

Field, Direskene – Roadside near Adada
19th Nov 2021

Direşkene was a particularly beautiful little village. From the relatively new, spaciously constructed mosque that marked the centre of the settlement, it was just possible to make out the valley I would be following for that day, set out in the crisp morning mist. Chickens chased each other through tumbledown houses, now their nesting grounds, whilst cattle wandered along the deserted roads periodically. The sunrise began to melt away the morning's mist as I set off again back down the hill to the tent. Keen to use up my remaining supplies of *sucuk* and white cheese before I risked them going bad, I had a huge breakfast, eating far more of the heavily salty meat and cheese than was comfortable, appealing, or remotely tasty.

My experiences of the trail from the day before, and the mess of missing and re-finding the path, led me to stick to the country roads for the morning. Once I reached the village of Siphaler, hopefully finding a shop to re-stock some food there, I would try the Way again. The morning's journey wound through pleasant country, mostly lined with pines and livestock fields on gentle slopes. Yet, periodically, the scene had been ruined comprehensively by roadside dumping. At one stage, the edge of the road was clouded out by a mixed detritus of discarded cans, sordid plastic bags, and rusting white goods. I was forced to tread carefully for a few minutes. I had seen similar in the mountains back in the other stages, but not had to physically walk through it before. Mercifully, such sections were short, but frustratingly common for a kilometre or so.

Still, they passed. The road wound lazily over a small dam, through further pine woods and past isolated, lone houses. Cattle sat on the roadside, watching sternly as I sauntered past, as if to question my presence in their territory. Rolling downwards as I crossed past the reservoir was a nice contrast to the slog up the day before. A few more turns and I came into Siphalier, making good time for once.

Siphalier had not only a small but well-stocked *bakkal*, but also an open tearoom. I bought two loaves of bread, for the next two days, and a few other bits for my lunch immediately. I ate far in excess of what was comfortable, again, but reasoned that it was better to refill properly whilst I could. I might not make it to another village that evening. Eating lunch outside the shop, the owner was clearly not sure what to make of me, but wanting to be welcoming, came to sit with me. After we'd covered off the standard conversation topics of family, work, and nationality, and I'd relayed as much as I was able to, he continued to sit with me in silence. I welcomed his gesture. A few boys spotted me finishing my haphazard meal, and gingerly wandered over to offer me *çay*. I accepted, not planning on being long. As I approached the teahouse, one of them leapt up to the vine growing over the doorway, plucked a full bunch of grapes from it, dropped back down to the floor, and handed them to me.

The tea shop itself was stiflingly warm from a traditional log stove in the middle of the room. On the wall, a poster detailed the names and reigns of past sultans of the Ottoman Empire, and the subsequent Presidents of the Republic, in one continuous narrative. I enjoyed my tea, but the boys' shyness got the better of them. Nonetheless, as I left, grapes in hand, the lads came out again to wave me off enthusiastically. As I left their happy little village, I still had the majority of the day left to walk.

Jumping back onto the Way offered a straighter, less hairpin-riddled route along the bank of the next valley. Committing to it, I left the tarmac road, and tacked up onto the west side, following the unreliable app. By and large, it was an exceedingly relaxing segment. Easy underfoot, without too many inclines, the afternoon was largely spent amongst the thick pines and soft forest floor, or on the gravel track that linked lone homesteads nestled in the hills. Bags of pinecones, gathered by an old lady I would spot occasionally, lay at the feet of a few trees. The valley became a crevasse, growing wider and deeper, becoming a more magnificent distraction as the afternoon ebbed along. It was difficult to track my progress, but for a while, it hardly mattered.

At one long, straight stretch, the peace was interrupted by a lone bark. The lone bark became several. I picked up a few egg-sized rocks. Three dogs began to work their way up towards me, emerging off the slopes of the valley onto my path. For whatever reason, I held onto the stones. I decided to be calm. If I threw, and they scattered, there was very little room to bypass them if they spread across the track. As I stood dead still, two of the less aggressive types got bored with the intruder, and padded along harmlessly. The third dog, a fairly large but domestic-like breed, stared on, barking constantly, creeping ever closer. Not wanting to upset a tactic that was evidently working, very slowly, I made my way round its side, before creeping, then walking, then determinedly marching, away. Bizarrely, it followed, causing me to continually turn around to stare it down, like a perverse game of 'Red Light, Green Light'. Eventually getting frustrated at the duration this thing had stolen off me, I lobbed a rock. The dog followed, but far enough away for me to stop caring.

As relaxing as the day had been, the sun was now very much dipping. I had been struggling to track just how far I had progressed, but had been given no options. When the path diverged dramatically, the question of where exactly I was became pressing. One trail lead down, unconvincingly through thick bushes, towards the riverbed. The other carried on uninterrupted, up along the valley's bank, but curving westwards on what felt, instinctively, to be the wrong direction. This was anything but 'good signposting'.

Dropping the pack and scouting the two options at a hurried jog, I decided the only option was to head down, towards the riverbed, bearing due south. It meant breaking with the clearly defined track, and hacking my way through dense undergrowth, only to reach the bed of a valley which might prove difficult to leave again. *Was there a path? Was there not?* Once I had hacked through dense undergrowth and slid down the steep embankment, all I really could rely on was a broad bearing, and the riverbed.

'Walking' downstream proved a misnomer. Once more, I was half scrambling, often jumping from boulder to boulder, to keep anything resembling a good pace. At one stage, I landed awkwardly, the momentum of the pack carrying me sideways. I stumbled as I steadied myself, and felt my ankle twist just a little too much to be comfortable. I stopped for a second, and swore at myself for being arrogant enough to try and cross the boulders that fast. Should I roll an ankle here, without signal, nearby roads, or anywhere remotely flat and stone-free to camp, I was utterly screwed. And so I slowed, picking between the boulders as best as I could, before reaching a flatter section of sandy riverbank.

Guessing at my whereabouts by now, I hacked up from the riverbed to see what I could make out from higher ground. Greeted by nothing but dense woodland, I was about to start hacking through, when I heard noises up ahead. I paused, instinctively ducking down behind a rock. Up ahead, a few black, silhouetted outlines were moving past me, at an angle. A small herd of boar, or at least something resembling black, furry pigs, were making their way along a badger trail. I froze. I had absolutely no clue as to whether boar were something to be worried about. Not wanting to find out, I crept back towards the river, sliding down the steep bank onto the stones again. Back on a flat-ish section of riverbed, I began walking downstream again, now making plenty of noise as I went. I wanted to avoid startling anything into a 'fight or flight' response, out here with no help at hand. If advertising my presence meant attracting anything aggressive, better to do so on the riverbed, where I could at least climb onto a boulder or two.

Twenty minutes more guesswork and cardinal directions continued, before I came to what appeared to be a tributary to the main river. I began scrambling up it, swiping through tree branches covering the stream bed, in the hope that blindly turning east for 200 metres or so would land me back on something like a road. Hurdling up a few dry waterfalls, ten minutes of slow progress later, a track appeared. It led south, straight up the hill in front in a step-like manner: steep ascent, plateau for twenty metres, repeat. As much as a path was good news, there was still absolutely nowhere to pitch nearby, I was still in the woods, and the brown ochres of leaves and bark were rapidly fading to greys and blacks. I started to run. Doing the inclines at a determined walk, and the flats at a run, was tiring work, but work I reasoned I could justify, getting close to the edge of the woods.

And then, the path banked steeply right, and vanished. There was a complete dead end, meeting a stream which snaked into impassable woodland to the left and right, and a solid wall of earth up ahead. I could make out little else in the rapidly fading evening light. I was still lost.

Satellite pictures seemed to indicate another thin, snaking route immediately west, directly up the bank through the woods, that headed south towards the road that I so desperately needed. Whether it was a path or not no longer mattered. Once more, the walking sticks were stashed behind the pack, and I started digging into the crusted layers of leaves and dirt with my bare hands. I was still recovering from the run up the ascent, but was not in the mood for staying here any longer than needed. Just as I had done the day before, I was back to all-fours progress up the bank, grabbing protruding roots for grip, strands of ivy clawing at the pack. Finally breaking out of the woodland again, once more exhausted, I stumbled onto what was, indeed, a track. The chalky trail now the only obvious guiding feature in the darkness, I could only manage a fast-walking pace for the final few minutes. After one last incline, the trees receded, and I met tarmac.

There was no time for the luxury of choice. I threw the tent down in a dirt-covered layby, facing a chicken-wire fence into someone's field. The occasional lorry steamed past, briefly illuminating the tiny scrap of roadside dirt I had claimed as home. I was next to what looked like a cattle shelter, just large enough for a tent inside. As tempting as it was to shelter from the strong wind, I dared not, in case I was woken at 03:00 by an inquisitive cow. Relieved to be metaphorically and physically clear of the woods, but without any water, or understanding of whose land I might be on, I awaited the morning nervously.

Day 52: 'The town around the hill'

Roadside near Adada – Clearing near Yeşildere
20ᵗʰ Nov 2021

I emerged at around 07:00. I was relieved that simply crashing on the side of the road hadn't offended anybody. Now on the summit of a small hill, the wind was no stronger than the night before, but bitingly cold. No amount of layers, comically stacked on top of each other around me, could quite subdue the shivering.

Without any water supply, I resorted to wandering down to a nearby farmhouse, hoping that I would be able to avoid hounding some poor family for water by finding a *çeşme*, tap, stream, or something along the way. I had no such joy. A woman in the farmhouse looked at me with intense curiosity. To my surprise, she didn't ask as many questions as I had expected, or frankly as many as I would have asked, but instead invited me inside, and handed me a ten-litre drum to begin filling from. I would have asked who I was, where I'd come from, and why I'd ended up in my front porch at just past seven in the morning. She felt no such need. Tremendously grateful, I made my way back, and rewarded myself with a whole two morning coffees, brewed up out of the wind in the cowshed, on a pile of straw (and likely dung). Small victories.

Packing down wasn't helped by the fiercely biting wind. Slowing down meant getting colder, which in turn lead to me slowing down, whilst the tent was halfway packed away. By the time I got away from the small patch of mud, I was grateful to be back on the road. Guttingly, I didn't have the time nor energy to stop off at the roman ruins I had been told so much about at Adada, now fifteen minutes off the track. Given that a lot of good memories had come from meanderings off the planned path, often to historical sites only accessible by foot, it was nothing short of negligent for me not to have found an extra half-hour in the day's plan.

The first village on the way, Sağlık, was tiny. A few builders working on a new mosque offered a hose, lying in the sand and cement of their site, as a water source. I happily accepted. I found the *bakkal* I had been told about, only to find it boarded up, closed years ago. When I asked a woman as to whether it was open at all that day, she answered no, but offered me anything I might need from it instead. With nothing pressing on my mind, and not wanting to burden her with requests, I thanked her and moved on.

The morning's route involved a lot climbing and descent, for which I kept my head down and ploughed through. I stayed on the main road mostly, but cut some distance off by re-joining the Way for a short segment. At about 12:00, the path dropped back down off the hills into the small town of Sütçüler.

Sütçüler was a fascinating little town. Had I co-ordinated my timings better, it would've been a good place to get a proper bed for the night. The town was really a few narrow streets, densely built around, winding their way across a few metres of elevation. The whole town wrapped itself in a band around the side of a mountain, like the residual high watermark left on a ship's bow. I was invited to eat with some construction workers, but I declined, seeking a full meal elsewhere. Arriving at a restaurant, I ate two weeks' worth of bread, lentil soup, *köfte* and cheese, getting my money's worth whilst I had the chance. Although served by a man and a boy that day, I was told it was owned by the woman behind the counter, who wasn't their mother or other member of their family. I stocked up on more food for the next few days, leaving my pack under their watchful care for half an hour.

Having resaddled the pack, I make a quick trip to a toilet in the basement of Sütçüler's mosque. It overlooked an idyllic square, not out of place in an English country town, which in turn looked out over the vast expanse of the valley below. It was only then that I realised that the mosque basement contained a small shower. It was probably a little indulgent, and definitely a waste of time, but half an hour later (and a lot cleaner) I re-started again.

Upon leaving, a group of students waved me over. They were studying at the campus of some far-off university in the tiny town. We exchanged social media details, and I think I ended up on a Snapchat story, if only in passing. I would have loved to have stayed longer, but finishing the day at 14:30 wouldn't have been justifiable. In hindsight, neither was attempting to cross through the next thirteen kilometres. Between Sütçüler and the next village, Çandır, the Way followed a trail through the Yazılı Canyon national park, running parallel to the main canyon in the hills on the southern side, via a tiny hamlet called Çürük. In the moment, I vastly underestimated just how much effort the next thirteen kilometres would demand, and set off down the hill.

The road out of Sütçüler wound heavily downhill. Once more the pressure on my knees and feet was a lot to bear, hairpin bend after hairpin bend. A herd of goats joined me at one segment, traipsing down in single file as Sütçüler receded into the past. Reaching the valley floor, the blinding, rapidly sinking sunlight made it almost impossible to keep staring straight ahead. To make matters worse, the mobile signal started to dip out, and I realised I had very little idea where the Way would leave the road. The Way's app still didn't work, Maps was all but useless, and none of my conversations in Sütçüler had indicated anyone had ever heard of the Way in the first place. I had to take a gamble, dropping off the road after rounding one of many rocky outcrops. The new road was at least vaguely towards where I hoped to be heading, purely by cardinal direction. Yet, it came to what looked like another dead end, meting out into a simple cemetery amongst the trees.

By this point, it was getting dark. There was no point trying to press onto Çandır, let alone Çürük, so I found somewhere to pitch. The only suitable place was by the side of the track, on a large pile of sand, discarded after long-finished roadworks had taken place. It took a little levelling to get to tent-pitching level. Whilst a shovel would've been useful, I made do with the side of a boot and a walking stick.

Falling asleep on the soft sand was very, very easy. I did so, however, under the preconception that I was somewhere near Çürük. Reality was far less comfortable.

Day 53: 'Nah'

Clearing near Yeşildere – Roadside, Yazılı Canyon
21st Nov 2021

On day 53, I woke up, and decided, "nah".

I would normally miss one or two alarms, getting off late as a result. But this morning, each successive snooze pressed led me to do so again. I had wholly run out of energy, or willpower, or something. As the morning wore on, a sense of fatalism killed any initiative I might have taken. *Getting up and starting to move again wouldn't matter now. You're too late,* I lied to myself, *so why bother?*

Getting up at 08:00 may not sound late, but it resulted in not starting the day's progress until gone 12:00. The sand that had been so comfortable to sleep on stuck to just about everything, taking forever to dust off. On the upside, I had a dry tent, and full batteries from the sunlight collected whilst I took too long. On the downside, I was now almost certainly behind schedule by a day.

It was only that morning that I started clocking the red and white patches daubed on trees, which I had seen before a few days back. It had taken me that long to realise that the Way worked in that manner. The 'route', if one could call it that, was so overgrown that no discernible path appeared, but 80% of the time a new red-white patch would be within sight. I spent the early afternoon scraping through a lot of harsh, thorny bushes, down into a dried riverbed, and up the steep incline on the reverse, following the red-white patches. It was hard going, and the midday sun was not the time to start striding up steep inclines, fully exposed. On my way up, preparing myself for a day of more hills, a man beckoned me over to chat. As we conversed, I was deeply annoyed to find out that this was not Çürük. Or at least, probably wasn't Çürük. Or probably anywhere near Çürük.

I was offered some food and water, and after hearing that I'm British, a WhatsApp video call with the man's son was hastily arranged. We chatted about football, briefly. Liverpool football club was a common talking point: by this stage, I was used to describing Liverpool as 'my team', which went down well, although in reality my family are far more strident followers than I. The man's garden was full of midges, and a higher-than-average number of cats lazing in the sun, but I was hugely thankful for his hospitality.

Passing his house, my disappointment partially ebbed. The red-white patches shone in the afternoon's sun, next to a clear path leading up into the thick wooded canopy of the canyon's national park. I was, somehow, on the right way. I made strong progress for a few hours, made better by the increasingly beautiful views off to my right. On a few occasions, there was nothing to be done but simply stop to pause and admire the landscape of the Yazılı canyon, stretching off far into the distance. Yet, nothing was going to change the fact that I was, severely, out of time today.

By distance alone, I figured that I could at least make it into Çandır, the village at the end of the canyon. However, when I arrived in a large clearing, in what seemed to be a tributary valley into the main canyon, things started to get seriously difficult. The Way's app, which gave me no information except the rough shape of the route ahead, seemed to take me up the side of a sheer cliff face. It directed me to leave the dirt track I was on, and dive straight up over the side of the next hill. Maps or satellite pictures gave no clues. Having run around trying to find any sort of lead, not even a badger path or set of footprints indicated a route in the direction instructed. I began to wonder if the current track had been built over the old Way, or it was far too overgrown, or if I was miles away from where I thought I actually was. Regardless, I was not going to be leaving the canyon today.

It took some serious running about, but after an hour or

so of searching, I was eventually able to find what I would have to follow the next day. The red-white patches started again, a hundred metres or so away from the track, but on the other side of a small rockfall. The original path was now most likely buried, but traversing across the strewn boulders, it was possible to pick up the red-white patches again. They in turn led up an incredibly steep path, which climbed into the hill in front of me like a giant's flight of stairs. It would be a tough climb, but that was a tomorrow problem. There was no way I could complete that this evening. It was better to rest, and attempt to tackle it properly the next day. I settled on making the small valley, still high up overlooking the main canyon, still fairly lost, my home for the evening.

As I was making camp, brushing loose stones away to clear a patch for the tent by the roadside, a car pulled up out of nowhere. The driver clocked my presence, but drove on, up into what I assumed to be a village of some sort to my south. As I was finishing pitching, the man with the car returned, along with two dogs who had harassed me from a distance earlier. He introduced himself as Huseyin, and seemed oddly interested in watching me pitch the tent. He has some faulting English, so communication was a joint effort. It turned out that the dogs belong to him, and were named 'Fındık' and 'Fiştik'.

I had been taught that the two words, used together, meant 'mixed nuts', which I found a lot funnier than I should've done.

Huseyin extended an invite to me to join him for drinks and a meal that evening, explaining that he had a house nearby. Now with an appointment to make, I made sure to wash in the freezing cold water of a stream, glad to feel clean again, before changing, and wandering up the road, into the pitch black. I left a small red flashing light atop the tent, and took a very precise note of the W3W location.

Arriving at Huseyin's house, I was greeted by Fındık and Fiştik, in strong voice as usual. Huseyin and his father-in-law have come to their very remote homestead-type place, to grill *sucuk* and *köfte*, eat snacks, and drink beers away from their alcohol-disapproving extended family. With our combined Turkish-English vocabulary, we were able to cover off a fairly extensive list of topics. We touched on a few political issues, and it turned out that, unfortunately, that they had some pretty objectionable views, which I pried into gently. Apparently, a lot of Turkish soldiers look up to Hitler ("as a superhero"), Israel is "very bad" because they persecute Muslims and "run the world", and Greeks are too, for killing Turks one hundred years ago. Despite there being "too many

Syrians" in Turkey, and the economy being pretty poor, Erdoğan is still a "good" leader. The Russians are "so-so", but a touch Islamophobic. Boris Johnson wasn't initially commented on, but I was reminded (as I always was) that he is Turkish. They enjoyed my crude impression of his Etonian drawl.

Curiosity getting the better of me, I ask what they thought of Meral Akşener: a former far-right politician who moved into more pro-European, liberal circles as her career progressed, and who I'd once written a few essays on at university. They both could tolerate the idea of her, despite coming from much further right on the political spectrum.

Outside of politics, I also learned that *Tuborg* was better than *Efes*, as the other major domestically brewed easily accessible beer, and I got a brief guide to some 'cultural' music from Youtube. Holding back from giving many of my own views on anything, I was just keen to try and understand their perspectives, however unpleasant at times. We eventually all enthusiastically agreed that some things, such as a love of fire, meat and beer, are common to men across all cultures.

I eventually retired, not wanting to outstay my welcome, and needing the rest. Having had a few beers and genuinely plentiful helpings of kebab meat, my offer of financial contribution was robustly rejected. They were most hospitable, and although were unable to help at all with understanding the route ahead, bid me safe travels for the next stages of the journey. I wandered back to the tent, a task made easy by the outstandingly clear moon, which bathed the entire scene in spectacularly bright moonlight. It was a temperate evening, the biting cold of the last few nights abating, for whatever reason. I slept very well, with a full belly.

Day 54: 'Crossing the dinosaur'

Roadside, Yazılı Canyon – Canlar Alabalık, Çandır
22ⁿᵈ Nov 2021

Day 54 would shape up to be one of the most difficult days of the entire journey. When trying to work out a sense of direction from about three different apps, I noted that on one of them, the steep hill I had encountered before looked a little like a dinosaur. My route bisected said dinosaur, and so that became how I mentally dubbed the day's work.

I woke early. The moonlight was still bright enough at six for me to start going about getting ready, so I was able to get something of a head start. The morning slowly ebbed from a moonlit golden hue to the white light of day. The whole canyon felt silently imposing, but there was a pristine beauty in being quite so far off the beaten track. There were few moments on the entire journey that were quite so peaceful.

Less fortunately, the noodles I'd brought a few days back turned out to be utterly inedible, so I started the day with only two mouthfuls of food. I set off in excellent time, for once, straight up the steep mountain path I'd found the day before, to begin 'crossing the dinosaur'. It was, once more, walking sticks away, hands in the dirt, scrambling work. Once more, the weight of the pack threw off my sense of balance, making for a few hairy moments as I hopped from boulder to boulder, the canyon floor getting further away with each step. Dragging so much weight up such an incline was thoroughly depleting work, and I rested frequently. Reassuringly, when stopping for breaths between bursts of energy, the red-white patches kept going. I like to imagine the painter carried less kit than I did. The path finally levelled out as I reached the crest of the hill, at which point I realised just how dramatic the drop had become. I looked straight down into the canyon for the most part, hundreds of metres below, obscured by thick pine cover.

The brief moment of easygoing did not last. Although only a few kilometres as the crow flies, and a few more with the added twists that the Way took, I spent most of the day on the same damned hill. The Way, and the red-white patches, simply did not follow any logical route, or any sense of distinction from the thick, prickly undergrowth. Time and time again, I would follow a path, only to miss the patches for a minute, only to find myself helplessly lost, unable to trace the last one. On several occasions I ditched the pack and ran through the dense trees on top of the hill, just trying to get a sense of where I was going. One time, I then lost the pack, resulting in no small degree of panic, as I scoured the top of the hill frantically searching for all of my kit. Just following a compass bearing was out of the question, as the cliff-edge curved south, presenting a real danger of losing my footing near the edge, and the thick, spike-adorned undergrowth limited visibility to a few metres in any direction.

Now, also out of proper food, and beginning to run out of light snacks, I was in a bind. That hill was one of the few occasions in which, although fought off, a small dose of panic began to set in. Progress all day was halting. Every metre had to be felt out by trial and error, and there was no counting the number of times I covered the same ground twice, sent the wrong way by a break in the trees that my mind construed as a path. It was hot, heavy work to do on no real food, and a rapidly depleting water supply. My underlying worry was that making it off the hilltop would be simply beyond me.

A breakthrough came after I, counterintuitively, followed the red-white patches north for a stretch, away from the overall direction of the Way, and found a steep but workable route along the cliff face. It led to a narrow path, which skirted along the top of the canyon for the remainder of my afternoon. At one stage, it required traversing around a protruding rock, and an old rope tied onto screws driven into the rockface was all that was provided for safety. Finally, the Way began the dive into the canyon.

It wasn't quite scrambling, but descending was once again hard work, as I struggled to keep the weight from carrying me down the hill. It was hard on my knees, hard on my feet, hard on every spot where straps, belts and harnesses had cut into my sides. I was determined now. I just wanted to get out of this canyon.

I bumped into two slightly overweight, middle-aged characters headed the other way.

"English?" "Nyet, Russki".

"Türkçe?" "Nyet."

With no common language, I bid them farewell in plain English. The couple's red faces looked baffled, but they cracked on up the hill I was breathlessly making my way down from.

I took a second to rest. As I sat down on the brown carpet of pine needles, I realised that they lay over a thick layer of grey ash, visible only if I brushed below the surface. A little way down the path, the tree trunks became steadily more charred and blackened, although their upper branches still appeared green and healthy. I recalled that, the year before, Turkey had suffered a series of horrific wildfires, and vividly realised that I was walking through the eventual aftermath of them. I felt more than a little humbled, as my boots steadily faded into the same ash grey colour with each step.

Finally, the path reached the canyon floor, merging with a track running parallel to the river. It was almost certainly not the best use of time, but after nothing short of a hot, prickly, worried day, I couldn't help myself. For fifteen blissful minutes, I allowed myself time to float in the crystal-clear waters, cascading straight from the hillside, as they carried off the day's worries. It was a very visible spot to strip off in, should another Russian couple have walked past. I couldn't have cared less.

In and out quickly, I followed the track out of the national park, emerging into what quickly felt tourist-tailored, friendly, and safe. Across the bank from a small open woodland kitchen, chainsaws, diggers and heavy machinery worked hard, pulling down the burnt husks of trees from the year before, as if they were tidying up dropped matchsticks. I enjoyed some freshly cooked trout, vegetables, and potatoes, before a young couple with a shiny red Audi invited me over to share some of their meal as well. They had prepared some *mıhlama* over a camping stove, and were sipping tea with it from a thermos flask, along with generous chunks of bread.

We got chatting. Between the three of us, we scraped together enough English – Turkish hybrid to communicate. She was a doctor, and he was a government worker of some description. They had come over from Izmir, and were heading along the coastline on a mini break together. For whatever reason, one of the first questions they asked me was, like the night before, about politics. I was, again, keener to hear what they had to say than to explain my own worldviews. But, once again, I was curious to ask about Akşener, as a juxtaposition to my hosts the day before. She seemed to resonate with this young, liberal, couple, too. Firsthand political research complete, I left the park, walking through yet more charred forests, and the remains of a few isolated, burned-out houses. Where they had once stood, all that remained was the charred stacks of chimneys, windowless concrete walls, and brick steps.

I came across a guesthouse of some sort just around the corner. Bizarrely, it was both a fish farm and a hotel, of some sort. Rooms overlooked enclosures of fish below, grown in water diverted from the river by a series of miniature aqueducts and pipes, which crisscrossed through the woods out of the park. I had many questions, but was far too tired for answers. I got the most basic room I could for the night, another fish-based meal for dinner, and called it an evening. I would have stayed a day to rest properly, but could ill afford to spend that much time after the delays of the last two days. Regardless, to be out of the hills, on a map once more, and in a proper bed, was all I could have asked for.

Day 55: 'Fair Enough'

Canlar Alabalık, Çandır – Next to a river,
Elmalıbük
23ʳᵈ Nov 2021

The following morning brought remarkable news. My
short segment of interview with the Fairbairn brothers
had made it onto their podcast. My voice was distant,
crackly, and I hated the answers I gave in hindsight. But it
was there. I lay back in bed, grinning to myself at the
conclusion of the amusing story, not quite believing it.

I had decided to ditch the Way once more, swapping
back to Maps, after a night of deliberation. There was
only a few kilometres difference between the Way, and
an actual road that I could see on Maps. Both led down to
the lake at Çandır, before following a valley up into the
hills, crossing over a watershed heading south, and
proceeding down towards the flat lands around Antalya.
By now, unless they would save me some serious
distance, I was in no mood to put my trust in the red-
white patches again.

I stepped off early, into a wet, cold morning. Dark clouds
hugged the mountaintops, obscuring the peaks, receding
as I got closer to the lake. More fish farms lined the river
down to Çandır, the river's water flowing constantly from
pool to aqueduct, into farms, and back again. I stocked up

on plenty of food, not wanting to be left without at least something to chew on again. By this point, I had begun to put larger, perishable items in a separate drysack, which clipped onto the (increasingly bulky) exterior of the pack, allowing me to carry more food in an accessible way. It was the culmination of a trend started nearly two months prior, in which the limits of how much I could carry inside the pack forced me to increasingly strap other kit onto it. Creative combinations of string and karabiners held sandals, spare clothes, solar panels, a towel, and now spare food all in place, with only the occasional mishap.

Leaving the village, true to form I wandered through another construction site, narrowly avoiding being run over by a roller compacting the side of the road. I spent the morning skirting the edge of the far-retreated lake, along a winding, pine-lined lane. Although at least the route was flat, the road wound around every small inlet, stream, and protruding rock, adding on a lot of ground to cover. The clouds refused to part all morning. Out on the water's edge, a few hundred metres away across the grey-turquoise mud, fish farming nets sat motionless on the dead-still surface.

The rough mid-point of the day, a tiny village on the lakeside called Kizilli, was desolately quiet. A few goats took shelter in a pen built into the side of a rock face, whilst yet more chickens wandered about freely. There was not a soul in sight. A lone stray was a little aggressive at first, evidently startled by my arrival, but after getting no response from me, settled back down into padding around aimlessly. It eventually wandered off, before returning with an old shoe, and flopping over for a nap.

After lunch, I began the move up into the hills. As I began to trek upwards again, ridges and peaks arising as I moved slowly up the valley, the clouds parted to reveal just how high the surrounding scenery rose. The peaks, crusted with the remnants of clouds, adorned the path I was taking out of grey, dull Çandır, and felt as though they were marking my progress as I continued. Somewhere, through this valley and over another set of hills, was the sea. Unable to find any name for it on maps, I mentally dubbed it 'good vibes valley'.

As I passed through a hamlet, an old man came out to greet me. I tried to make conversation, complimenting how beautiful this area was, only to get nods and grunts in return, the man saying absolutely nothing. He seemed happy enough, despite welcoming me non-verbally, so I cracked on, winding slowly up good vibes valley. The dull trampling of hooves in mud from a herd of cows a field over was the only sound that broke the silence.

As the afternoon wore on, the grey lakeside clay turned

to thick, maroon mud underfoot. The clouds re-descended: as I got higher, they crept down from the distant peaks lining the way, to the winding path that I trudged upwards on. A family helping their mother drag fallen branches down the path were some of the only people I saw all day. We exchanged nods and left each other to our work. Further on, a tiny, yappy dog ran up to me, and refused to re-join its increasingly impatient owner.

Realising how short on time I was, again, I re-adjusted my plans. It would be impossible to get out of the valley by the end of today, so I set my sights on reaching the small village nestled on the brook, Elmalıbük. I had to seriously pick up the pace, as the track began to meander down, deeper into the valley. The gentle sound of the call to prayer, echoing mournfully across the hills, distant through layers of fog and cloud, made me realise how rapidly time was escaping.

Perhaps I came across a bit too directly, or simply looked sketchy after 55 days on the move, or simply failed to adequately explain what I was doing. Regardless, the only individual I came across at the entrance to Elmalıbük rebuffed any suggestions I had as to locations to camp nearby. The village was tiny, with little more than a small mosque and a few smallholding houses dotted around a quiet brook. Not that I could have known in advance, but there was no small shop, or anything like a place to resupply. A little panicked given the rapidly dimming light, I passed through the village at a forceful pace, and once clear of the houses, began looking for a safe, secluded spot. If you can't get permission, don't ask for it.

After a little searching, I found a flat patch of mud nestled under a tree. It was a relatively well-hidden position, blocked off from two directions by rocks, and a third by the stream. I dragged branches and loose foliage across the final side to further hide the tent's outline, just in case. Although I hadn't hit my targets for the day, I had made good progress. Now, with a river, enough food from that morning, and a place to rest, I was in a good place for the next day. It was a wholly uneventful night.

Day 56: 'Mud.'

Next to a river, Elmalıbük – Roadside near Bağbellen
24ᵗʰ Nov 2021

As lovely as it is to wake up to the sound of rain on canvas, particularly when you're warm and dry, it only lasts until you have to put the tent down. Sure enough, this proved a nightmare. The soft red earth that made for a comfortable night's sleep turned into thick sludge of maroon mud, which clung to everything. Everything grew heavier, as the tent, my immediate layer of clothes, the pack, and all the protective wrapping I had kept everything in up until now, was dyed a thick, dark cherry colour.

The day started on an immediate uphill. Trudging up into the hills through the light but constant drizzle was heavy, exhausting work, soaking my thin walking shirt and trousers in both sweat and rain. I was faced with near-constant elevation all morning as I sought to climb over what, in theory, should be the last day of heavy inclines. The walking sticks began to soften, being exposed to the constant mud and damp, as each meander around the hills took more energy than the last one to summit. The fog only got thicker as I marched higher into constant cloud, losing visibility metre by metre. I crested the first incline, that which got me out of the main valley, after a morning of slow progress. Relieved to have finished one incline, the forest broke into open fields, a small village, and a brook running through the centre. I realised, more than a little shocked, that I had crossed into the final province of the walk. I was now, finally, in Antalya. I had lunch by a small stream in the tiny village of Kızılçukur, taking shelter from the gentle rain under a rock. It was a cramped way to relax, but I felt grateful to be out of the elements for at least fifteen minutes. Flocks of sheep let themselves out to graze, migrating slowly across the hilltop as tiny white flecks by their own accord. They looked warm. I was envious.

Moving on, I had just begun to mount the next, final incline, when a lone old man called me over to ask what I was up to. The first person I had seen all day, I was grateful for the brief conversation as I passed through his hamlet. Despite my very soggy state, he was kind enough to invite me in for tea. I struggled to pull off my sodden, mud clogged boots, before following him upstairs, into the first floor of his home. He was a quieter gentleman than many, dressed in the usual cardigan and shirt common to Turkish men of his generation. He finished praying in the corner of the living room whilst I sat, not quite sure where to look to afford him some privacy, and his wife began to bring through *çay*. She staggered

298

around, an older individual like him, but stayed entirely bent double at all times, bringing through generous quantities of cheese, *pekmez*, local honey, and bread. I was tremendously appreciative, and ate as much as I dared without overstaying my welcome. I was happy to break from my standard died of simple bread, cheese and whatever I could brew on a camping stove. I tried not to stay too long, intensely conscious that finding anywhere to stay in the hills was a difficult task. They were kind in understanding my sense of urgency, and came outside to wave me off along with their chickens, as I jumped back on the track that lead ever southwards.

After their house, the last serious incline of the entire journey began to bite. More endless winding through thick woodland set in. Often each hairpin would double back on itself, taunting me as if I hadn't actually travelled very far at all. I felt cheated. The clouds got thicker as I climbed again, but the weather held, until I reached the summit of the hill. There, the heavens truly opened. I hoped desperately that the waterproof cover I'd wrapped around my pack was working, and leant into the sideways-blown rain. A lone Turkish flag hung in a tree, somehow clinging onto the branch it was tied to, despite the winds now doing their best to take the whole branch off. One hundred metres, and three more hairpin bends later, I arrived in the tiny hamlet of Bağbellen.

I had hoped forlornly that a guesthouse existed in the village. Sometimes luck was on my side, Maps was right, and such isolated beacons of hope did exist. As I topped the final incline of the journey, bracing myself against a signpost as the full force of the ridge's weather hit square in the face, I realised that today was not a lucky day. Nothing but a wall of cloud, stinging raindrops, and five lonely houses greeted my arrival. Not wanting to narrowly miss somewhere, I asked at a nearby house if there was any sort of hotel or *pansiyon* nearby. An old woman answered, confirming there was no such place, but she refused to let me pass without coming inside to dry off, and to have some *çay*. I obliged.

Çay, over the course of an hour or so, turned into the chance to dry off my soaked outer layers over a roaring stove. As much as I knew I would be heading back out into the elements, the family insisted I hang my sodden walking shirt over their stove. I was lent a hilariously oversized, garishly bright, pink Hawaiian shirt in the meantime. Sat in front of a huge flatscreen TV, I tried to make best sense of the 24-hour rolling news, and was served what turned into a full meal of chickpea soup, breads, cheese and tomatoes, and a lot of *çay*. My conversation with the woman's extended family, all of whom were relatively senior in age and lay slumped into deep armchairs, was halting, but I did my best to try and

300

be sociable. I must have looked ridiculous.

Once the rain eased off, I got back on the road again. The clouds had parted enough for me to vaguely discern that I was on the top of a very high ridge, although I couldn't make out much further than that. My plan to make it to the next village on the road was, characteristically, over-ambitious. As darkness set in, I found myself running about again, looking for a source of water, and failing to find one. Nevertheless, I was able to throw the tent down on a soft patch of earth, concealed from view by a few rocks, at the edge of another woodland. I was a little apprehensive about what might be lurking further in, but I was beyond caring now. It was, at least physically, all downhill from here.

Day 57: 'When the horizon became flat'

Roadside near Bağbellen – Clearing near Akçapınar
25ᵗʰ Nov 2021

The next morning was, mercifully, very warm. I took some time out of my usual routine to let the tent dry, the red mud of the last two nights turning a dull ochre. I could clean it properly later. It only needed to last another few days.

A small rocky outcrop, sat atop a hill, tempted me briefly. My hunger for things to climb, just to run up to prove it could be done, was still just as strong as before. I eschewed it, however, for desperate want of making progress. I was, at most, no more than seventy-two hours away from finishing. The temptation to thrash myself to the finish, to try and run the next seventy kilometres to the sea, collapse in a heap, and be done with the whole thing, was powerful.

About half an hour into making progress downhill, the all too familiar side-side motion of holding oneself back down a hill already beginning to pressure my joints, I was met by a break in the treeline to my right, and the first real long-range view to the south for a few days. The luscious pine forest carried on for miles, revealing that the hills sloped steeply down onto flatter, brown-orange farmland far below. Far into the distance, however, the hills stopped. For the first time in two months, looking south did not yield another skyline or another boundary to cross. The horizon became completely flat. Only a razor thin sliver of blue sat in their place.

Right on cue, I got mobile signal back, having not been able to communicate for a few days. As I plodded further downhill, slaloming through endless forest, two cars drove the other way. One was a *jandarma* police vehicle, and the other a civilian pickup. The latter vehicle stopped, and a window was rolled down for me. The owner asked what I was up to, and I gave the customary spiel, but with a little more energy and enthusiasm than normal, with the finishing line in sight. He invited me to come find his place for food someway down the road.

The knees kept taking the punishment of continuous downhill through the endless forest. I was wise to not have pressed onto the village of Bozdoğan the day before, as it turned out to be little more than a cluster of derelict homes, and seemingly empty homesteads. A few small yappy dogs turned up, and then beat a rapid retreat. I knew what I was doing by now. Once the mid-afternoon arrived, I had broken out of the pine tree line, although not out of the woods yet. Immediately reaching a grove of olive trees, with the sun beating down straight into my vision, my arrival in the tiny village of Kozan felt like far more of an achievement than I had expected it to. After a great deal of frustrated searching for this restaurant (which I was certain was real by now), I resorted to asking a local. He pointed straight across his land and through his hedge, so I obliged, following a tiny path through what felt like someone else's farm.

I was greeted at a small homestead by a woman, who went to immediately prepare another meal of fish, bread, fries and vegetables. Chickens ran freely throughout their small compound, and a tiny, yapping dog tried my patience as much as it could. At one stage, it made off with one of my socks as it lay drying in the sun, which I only recovered after a short tussle. When the food came, as I often did, I helped myself to a lot more bread than my host was probably anticipating, stocking up on carbs for the rest of the day's work.

As I was finishing, the man who had driven past earlier returned, with the two *jandarma* officers, and they ordered the same. The man, who seemed to be the head of the group, told me that the dog's name was 'Joe Biden'. I joked that the dog could not possibly be called Joe Biden, as it was *"moving too fast"*. My audience found this hysterical, and so emboldened, I carried on. My host asked if maybe they should get a Trump dog. I pointed to a chicken and said something about both Trump and it being orange, which my audience also found highly amusing. I have never surpassed this level of linguistic ability. I probably never will.

The owner of the whole place offered me a room for the evening, in one of a number of small chalet-type wooden huts, but I was desperately keen to try and make it out of the woods entirely. I decided to return to the Way, in the hope that it would shave off a few kilometres by heading cross-country. So once more, I re-joined the sporadic trail of red-white patches, and after being led directly through a newly constructed farm, was more or less able to follow the others successfully. Each time I passed another patch, I would reach out with a stick and tap it, a habit I picked up in Çürük. It was partially for luck, and partially so I couldn't physically wander too far off again.

The path dived off into the undergrowth, so it was pretty hard to deviate from the set route. For the most part, I was following a small stream, which grew as the sea beckoned closer. The Way tunnelled through thick vegetation, crossing over and around the brook as it wound further down through the hills. It was easy to pause along the course of the stream. A group of turtles lounged about in the sun, quickly scattering as I approached, diving beneath the perfectly clear water. At another pool, I paused to wash my face and hair at the waterfalls near Uçansu. As tempting as it was to jump in again, I had progress to make. The path was heading, mostly, due south. Every step I was taking felt like, at last, it was actually taking me closer to the end of the journey. I had a new sense of momentum. A renewed appreciation of urgency gripped me.

Determined to get every little bit of distance out now, whilst I felt energetic enough to push myself, I started running again. Just as I had done on the night-time bolt through to Çukurca, I ran small downhill segments, before pacing out the flatter areas. The tiny path wound through thick evergreen forests, curving around and over the tiny brook. Finally, it came to the base of the hill, joining a wide forest track, and flattening out entirely. Not thinking much of it at the time, I had unwittingly come off the final hill of the whole journey. Only a vast expanse of flat forests, fields and farms lay between me and the sea.

Now exhausted, and having thoroughly soaked a pair of cotton trousers in heavy sweat, the last few kilometres were surprisingly tough. The thick mud on the forest track, churned up by constant vehicle use, stuck to my boots in great clumps. Every few paces, it would need scraping off in some form just to keep going. Now walking alongside a full river rather than a brook, the meanders became more dramatic on the flat ground, adding distance at every turn. What would have been great fun to drive, was hard work to trudge along, each wide meander pushing me further away from the finish line.

My original day's intent had been Akçapınar, a large village just clear of the forest I was still in, marking the final transition into farmland. True to form, come 17:30, it became obvious that this not going to be feasible. However, as I was only dropping short by a kilometre or so, and I had found an ideal spot to pitch in, I wasn't concerned. I had found a large clearing, covered in a firm but gentle bed of moss and grass, around which rows of beehives were dotted. A small row of pines covered me from view from the track, and the river was easy to access, its waters flowing crystal clear over polished stone only fifty metres away. The only significant factor was what appeared to be a long-abandoned graveyard nearby, the tiny headstones encrusted with thick lichen and covered in trees. Trying not to disturb any resting souls, I had a wholly uneventful evening. I slept well, eagerly anticipating the next day's progress out of the woods, at last.

Day 58: 'Not out of the woods yet'.

Clearing near Akçapınar – Roadside, Kurşunlu
26ᵗʰ Nov 2021

My idyllic camping spot made a slow morning somewhat inevitable, reluctant as I was to actually get up and go. The only major issue I had begun to struggle with was, in conjunction with a lack of mobile signal, a lack of power for the phones. I desperately tried to get the solar panel to work with the first drops of sunlight that filtered through the trees, but it was slow going.

The silence was broken in an instant. Three dogs, the first a small, yappy creature but the other two larger animals, appeared only twenty metres away, barking at the top of their lungs. They had no owner in sight. Presuming the worst, I picked up a few stones, finding only pathetic little pebbles in the moss, and threw the first at the tiny animal. Absolutely nothing happened. The yapping and barking continued, and all three edged closer. I threw another at the smaller dog, flying just past its head. The dog was undeterred. I grab a stick, and wondered what exactly to do next.

At that point, their apparent owner arrived. Inexplicably, he came from the direction of the river, perpendicular to the only track nearby, before moving off into the woods through the abandoned graves, following no apparent direction. He said nothing about his dogs, my presence, my half-flattened tent, or any of the frankly surreal scene unfolding in front of us both. Equally inexplicably, five minutes later, a tiny, corgi-like creature ran after him, into the dark hues of the woodland.

After this scene, I set off down the track once more. I was desperately keen to regain signal or sunlight to work out just how far exactly remained to go. I pushed myself to get past the winding meanders as quickly as I could, leaving the woods just shy of Akçapınar in an hour. Bright sunlight and flat fields greeted me, for as far as I could see. Ironically, it was only here, after my end goal had dropped out of sight again, that I truly appreciated just how much ground I was going to have to cover in the next three, or if I was lucky, two days.

The morning was spent working through seemingly endless fields of fruit trees. As much as I was trying to speed up, to cover as much ground in the daylight hours as possible, it was a somewhat relaxing start to the day. The same mini-aqueducts I had seen up in Çandır, made of concrete half-pipes laid end to end along the roadside, provided a ready source of drinking water all morning.

The exhaustion began to set in at around midday, as the sun beat down aggressively, and I tried to find an open bridge across the Aksu river. As I tried to make my way around, some large, unhappy-looking dogs began following me, visibly agitated by my presence. At this stage, I was too tired and too irritated to yield to them. I picked up stones, and began throwing, scattering the animals each time a rock sailed closely by its target. One particularly persistent German shepherd was keener than the others, but didn't even get close to me. I was used to this by now, and took a little joy in finding heavier rocks to hurl at them, hoping one might actually find its mark. As I left them behind, getting over the bridge, something about mad dogs, Englishmen, and the midday sun sprung to mind.

After doing so, I took a few minutes to take stock. I was once more under my own direction, having left the Way as it continued due south, to make my own way south-west towards the city of Antalya itself. A small part of me contemplated hacking due south, just to get to any beach whatsoever and call it quits, but I cracked onto my original target, the north-most point on Konyaaltı beach in the centre of town. I had long dreamt of touching down on that one particularly stony beach in the centre of the city. It had become something of a symbol of completion, built into my mind over the last two months. I was transfixed on reaching that tiny, tourist-teeming corner of the city, even if it added on a few extra miles. And so, my new route would take me straight through great swathes of greenhouse-covered farmland, before actually reaching the city proper.

Consequently, the remainder of the day was hot, hard work, in which I saw very few people. The only real human contact came from the owner of an occasional store, and a group of Syrian migrant workers, who were particularly friendly. Their one Turkish speaking friend took lead, whilst the two others and I tried our best to get by with gestures and smiles. Having heard so many negative stories about the number of Syrians flooding Turkey, I was glad to finally meet some, who enthusiastically began telling me about their jobs in the fields around. The group offered to help me onto a bus going the right way, but I explained that I had already completed so far on foot, and I would finish in the same way. Nevertheless, watching my new-found friends board a bus for the city, completing in half an hour a journey that would take me over twenty-four hours of graft, was painful to watch.

My thought process on where exactly to end up for the evening was confused, and I wasn't thinking straight. At one stage, I planned to smash out 17 kilometres, through the night, to get to the closest AirB&B, just to avoid camping once more. About an hour later, hobbling along at around 16:00, I scrapped the plan as too ambitious. Another advertised hotel, true to form, failed to exist outside of a map.

I sensed that the sea of greenhouses and farms might make it difficult to find an undisturbed, concealed spot, so I tried to press onto the large wooded national park that was in the right direction. Falling short of that, I ended up in yet another small woodblock next to a road. Conscious that wild camping is one thing in the hills, but another altogether in suburban Antalya, I constructed two screens of branches to break up the shape of the tent once more. Darkness having fallen, being told to move on was simply not an option. I was able to get more bread and cheese from a nearby shop. The owner couldn't care less who I was, or where exactly I had materialised from.

Lack of power for the phones was still a real issue. Not wanting to get lost in the sign-less sea of greenhouses and farms the following day, I made a rough mental note of my direction of travel, and where to leave which road. The identikit maze of white plastic and tracks, without clear signage or many people to talk to, could only end badly unless I was careful. Trying to drift off to sleep, for the first time since starting, it was uncomfortably warm.

What I had failed to factor into my location for the evening, however, was precisely who my neighbours now were. I had placed myself adjacent to a large dog kennels. At around 23:00, the howling started. One dog would start, the others would join in eagerly, until silence descended. Another would start, the cycle would start again, the whole complex opening up in chorus, like the ripple of musket fire on a faraway hilltop. They were annoying at first, but I figured it was safe. They were behind a wire, surely. Then, the sounds of barking started getting closer.

By now, I was prepared to see more wild/stray dogs at the edges of major cities. In the complete wilderness, very little refuse existed for strays to feed off, whereas in the city centres they were kept under control. It was always the small towns or liminal edges of cities where packs became emboldened enough to cause problems. The periphery of Antalya would prove to be the worst. For hours, well into the early morning, several packs of dogs ran wild through the fields and trees. They would get closer to my tent, ominously getting louder, before receding, only to return when those in the sanctuary began howling again. At one stage, they got so close that the distinct sound of one shaking its head, its wet tongue and cheeks hitting one another, came only a few metres away. Then the sounds would recede, I'd drift off a little, only to be reawoken again. Each time, I'd grasp the hammer I had kept as a weapon a little tighter, for the little good that it would do, knowing full well there was no one nearby to come and help.

They went on, maddeningly, for hours. I didn't sleep until gone 03:00, with one ear very much open.

Day 59: 'Fin'

Roadside, Kurşunlu – Konyaaltı Beach, Antalya
27ᵗʰ Nov 2021

I was constantly looking over my shoulder as I packed up the tent. Mercifully, none of the wild dogs from the night before made an appearance. The second tin of camping gas finally ran out, just when I needed it to. Nevertheless, despite a groggy, drizzly start, the trees showering the tent and I with every gentle breeze, there was a spark in what I was doing. I was going home.

As I stepped out of the woodblock, the drizzle turned to light rain started almost immediately. There was little point in putting on waterproofs now. I started down the road, my thin walking shirt and trousers soaked five minutes in, and soon entered the national park I'd tried to reach the night before. There wasn't much to see.

My first stop was in a large, newly constructed mosque, adjacent to an enormous, newly finished cemetery. It had been carved out of the trees, and stretched on for a good kilometre or so, grave after grave on end. The large mosque was all but deserted, save a few individuals not doing particularly much. I walked on confidently, as if I had reason to be crossing half a construction site in the process. A memorial wreath to a sunken submarine, I

315

believe, lay sodden on a slab of concrete. The huge, imposing doors to the mosque were guarded by two filthy black dogs, who lay idlily by on the stone. Happy to see me, one with a swollen, infected eye padded up, as if to welcome me. Stepping into the mosque, I put the two phones on to charge for a bit. It was that, or (in the absence of any sun to solar charge from) get hopelessly in endless white greenhouses later. I knelt down, and took a second to thank God, regardless of his name.

A few kilometres on, I was able to grab an early lunch at a place clearly designed for tourists, nearly deserted in late November. I had a fairly unremarkable meal of *köfte*, bread and the like, not wanting to hang around. By this stage, drenched, stinking and heavily bearded, I was lucky to have been served. Moving out of the national park, six ragged dogs eyed my walking past, but remained aloof. Further down the line, a huge *kangal*, clearly not pleased to see me, trotted towards me. Thoroughly tired of dogs by now, I grabbed one of my walking sticks by the end, and swung it in a wide arc behind me. It caught the dog straight on the side of the face, the thick stump making contact with a satisfying smack. Defied, the *kangal* slunk away, head bowed, silenced. The threat was now obviously void, but after two months of continual alertness and dog-related frustrations, I was happy to finally make contact with one, and watch it pad away, defeated. Alone, except for the dog, I screamed a string of obscenities in its wake.

Finally leaving the thick woods of the park, I crossed a large dual carriageway, and found myself immersed in greenhouse land. For the next eight kilometres, no navigational aides stuck out, no views were admired, and there was nothing to guide me. I ended up hopelessly lost once or twice, once wandering straight up someone's driveway, trying to walk through their property before being very politely corrected. The morning was mentally draining in a way unmatched by other physically difficult segments. The feeling of having already covered a good deal of ground, and facing only more, with no indication of progress, 'end point' or guide to how much was left, made it an unexpectedly challenging segment.

And then, it began tipping it down. Finished with the gentle showers of the morning, it began unreservedly pouring, as if sensing that I was nearing the end. Wet through to the skin, my phones bundled together hastily in a waterproof bag, the wind began to chill me throughout. I sought shelter under the slight overhang of someone's roof. They wandered out and past me, in full waterproofs, and angrily beckoned for me to get off their front patch of dirt. This would be the first and last time I was told to go away. It was fully within overhang man's right to tell me so, but stepping back out into the lashing, unrelenting rain, I was particularly annoyed at. Relenting after five minutes, the next time the heavens opened I sought shelter in an industrial greenhouse, listening to the heavy rain from under the white plastic sheeting, kept company by a few thousand tomatoes.

Greenhouse land was, sure enough, a nightmare to try and pick my way through. At another stage, I was led through a field of thick, sticky red mud, in hindsight probably belonging to someone, only to find a closed gate on the other side. I was able to un-twist the thick steel wire holding it shut, haul it open, and do a hashed job of re-wiring it shut, before the next downpour started. As greenhouses merged into faceless, anonymous surburbia, one lane was entirely covered in a foot of water after the day's downpour, resulting in what felt like endless doubling back, and trial and error. By the fourth downpour, I stopped bothering to look for shelter, and embraced being totally saturated from socks to shirt. It couldn't last forever. At last, after what felt like eternity, the rows of concrete bungalows opened up into a vast open patch of dirt, littered with industrial detriutus. Beyond it, lay the highway into the city.

It was a dead-straight march through semi-industrial wasteland, unchanging for kilometre after kilometre.

Some distance along the way, I was invited in for *çay* by a number of men outside their shop. Well supplied with very sweet *çay*, I conveyed the excitement of being so close to finishing. They understood my anticipation, except one, who (ever true to form), only wanted to ask why Britain supported Israel as much as it apparently does. When someone suggests I might like a biscuit or two, I was duly offered several packets, entirely for free, despite my protest. Having dried off around their fire, and with an excessive number of chocolate biscuits consumed and acquired, they wished me well, and I jumped back onto the endless brick pavement. To my left, the tower of Antalya airport was just visible through the low clouds. Beyond it, the wild sea beckoned. I resisted the temptation to tack due south. Twelve kilometres to go.

Another mentally challenging segment followed. Nothing but discarded rubbish, piles of dumped concrete, and failed, empty building sites sat along the nigh-deserted four lane highway. It in turn stretched back behind me, a paved, luxury route to nowhere. A child hitched a lift on the back of a pickup as it stopped at some lights, the driver wholly unaware.

The sun was setting by the time I crossed a bridge across the river Duden, marking my entry into the city itself. Navigation stopped being as simple as 'go that way', as all the recognisable sights, smells and sounds of a city appeared. The end was tentatively close now. Antalya became a busy city, dizzyingly quickly, as I crossed the first few junctions. I was nine kilometres from the sea.

The weather, not content with giving me such an easy ride, opened up in one last downpour. Having now been soaked and re-dried at least twice through, I rolled on. To the bemusement of drivers, local shop owners sheltering under their facades, and the pedestrians caught under bridges waiting for the downpour to stop, the site of me walking through the solid mass of rain was probably quite odd. It seemed to sit in a thick layer across the road, soaking everything up to one's knees in splash, held there by the glaring lights of the evening's rush hour traffic. I waded on through, but the day's exertion was catching up with me.

I stopped for one final break at a tiny street kitchen, and sheltered under a thin tarpaulin held in place by wooden beams, as I had myself a kebab. I couldn't care less what was in it. The staff found my halting language, thoroughly soaked demeanour, and enormously unwieldy pack, plain funny. I probably would have done too.

The last six kilometres weren't quite the hardest. By this stage in the day, my initial energy and momentum was well worn through. Slogging out the last stretch along the main highway in Antalya, in a sea of bright lights, glamorous locals and glaring traffic, the overwhelming emotion was one of incredible isolation. The experiences of the last two months, all held together, simply didn't make sense here. All I could think of was rest, the finishing line no longer even a desirable target now. I simply wished to stop. A few times along the way, my feet simply couldn't take any more, and I took brief rests in bus shelters along the central strip. Young people around my age, decked out in black designer gear, sheltered from the gentle drizzle with me, occasionally looking this smelly stranger up and down in pure disbelief, until a taxi pulled in.

Finally, the left turn I was after, came along. Diving in-between the sea-side apartments, I was suddenly faced with a black, empty void. Away from the cars, the sound of waves crashing on rocks could be heard. A few locals made use of the clubs and bars between me and the edge of the sea, but being out of season, and hardly a pleasant evening, I imagined it was quiet for a Saturday.

The final few steps, to my surprise, weren't exciting. I had played out the scene of reaching the beach time and time again mentally, holding it out in my mind as a trophy to grasp for, whenever the going got tough. Bizarrely, I had assumed I'd be arriving on a sunny afternoon, as if I hadn't finished each other leg in darkness after an unusually tough day. I made my way down the winding road to the beach. Wandering past what I took to be a 'no entry' sign for the sailing club that occupied that plot of seafront, I stepped gingerly onto wooden decking.

At 20:40, precisely, I hit shingle. Nothing but the sound of the waves greeted me. Actually setting foot in the water proved to be a lot trickier than in Kefken, and I succeeded only in soaking my boots and feet through. As when I set off, I felt a hymn was an apt way of marking the moment. I mumble the words under my breath to 'The Day Thou Gavest', and gazed out into the thick black clouds lurking above the Mediterranean.

As the hymn ended, a lone cat trotted past behind me. A few local students sat on the beach, laughing, throwing stones at the swell. I was left to gaze into the foaming mass of the waves, the horizon stretching flat and empty into the void.

70: Morning in Direşkene.

323

71: The tea shop, Sipahiler.

72: A home along the St Paul's Way, south of Siphalier.

73: Following the St Paul's Way southwards, whilst the path still existed, south of Siphalier.

74: Sütçüler, the town built around a hill.

*75: The view out across the canyon. Candır lake can be seen in
the distance.*

76: The reality of 'crossing the dinosaur', as visibility reduced to near-zero for much of the day.

77: Wildfire damage in Candır.

78: 'Good Vibes Valley', south of Candır.

79: Crossing into Antalya province, bedraggled.

80: My first glimpse of the sea in two months.

81: Arrival on the beach, Antalya.

333

Conclusion: *"Neden?"*

Had this account been a fictional novel, the task of drawing the journey to a close on Antalya's shoreline would have been quite daunting. The overwhelming weight of emotion associated with finishing the journey, that I had so eagerly anticipated before and during the venture, would have made crafting the 'ideal' ending a real challenge of descriptive power.

In reality, the only sensation that filled my mind as I came to a steady halt after two months of endurance, was just how ordinary the moment felt. There was no sudden realisation of accomplishment. There was no deep, meaningful, life-changing epiphany that became suddenly apparent on the shingle. There was no moment of divine revelation, personal enlightenment, or whatever it was I was half-expecting to fall from heaven. I did not, as the stereotype of a youngster on his travels might say, 'find myself'.

There were lessons that were apparent immediately after I had finished. They came in pieces, jotted down as I packed my things, took a 04:00 taxi to Antalya's airport, and began re-integrating myself into 'normal' life. I learnt that, even with the most interesting task and purpose ahead in the day, my mornings remained obstinately slow. I stayed lazy, despite knowing that doing so would result in less time spent exploring off the trail, less time resting, less time talking to folk, a higher risk of injury and burnout, and far less tales to recount later.

Aspects of that laziness were apparent elsewhere, too. Had I completed the trip again, ensuring I was equipped with a much higher standard of Turkish would be a much higher priority. My weakness when conversing outside of a few topics meant that my 'comfort zone' became very clearly defined. I could do the initial 'where are you from' interaction; a few details about my family and their livelihoods; where I was going that day, in the next week, and overall; my tent, food, clothing and other daily concerns; and that no, I was not married, had no girlfriend, and had no intentions of acquiring one on the way. I would occasionally go beyond this, and come away from such halting, awkward interactions with a great sense of pride. Yet, it became all too easy to fall back onto the same well-versed lines, nodding my way through whatever response came back. I should have continued to challenge myself linguistically, visiting more settlements and talking to more people where geography allowed. As difficult as some such scenarios were, they produced the best memories. Had I guarded more vigilantly against getting lazy, and been better prepared linguistically, there is no doubt that this book would have been longer.

Yet, that same lack of preparation added an invaluable appreciation of the unexpected. Finishing this memoir fourteen months after completing the journey has only amplified in my mind how amateur an effort it really was. In the absence of actual printed maps, all navigation was done from a beaten-up old iPhone. My boots were simply the closest pair I had to hand, plus a few new socks. Hung together by spare boot laces, duct tape and creatively tied knots, the trip had stood as an ode to amateur effort. It stands as an ode to accepting a level of tolerable risk, and therefore an acceptable level of tough nights, social awkwardness, and physical pain. It is is an ode to my skittish, mildly terrified younger self, dismounting a coach in Taksim square with bags strapped awkwardly to his front and back, already hopelessly lost before even starting the walk.

That 'amateur effort' aspect was only partially reflected in my avoidance of overly rigid planning: as the trip progressed, this became more by design than by accident. Working within a loose guide of each stage's distance and elevation, broken down into three or four day 'best and worst case' plans whilst on the road, afforded the best compromise between getting across the country and enjoying it as I went. Whether exploring the ancient caverns of Çukurca, stealing quick swims in as many lakes or rivers presented themselves, or running up unnamed hills simply for the hell of it, the lesson was clear. It was the un-designed, the spontaneous, and often impractical, that fully brought to life the pristine freedom of living on the road.

That space for the unexpected was key to fully appreciating the hospitality and kindness offered by so many. I had heard and read about such a culture before, but it is impossible to accurately gauge something as subjective as an attitude or feeling. Although I have done my best to describe the kindness of strangers, such a sensation is impossible to fully grasp without names, faces and stories. It is one thing to have heard of Turkey's culture of hospitality. It is another entirely to remember Yusuf the foreman; Faruk and his family; Hasan the logistician and Hasan the goat herder; Mustafa and his tea shop; and Huseyin, his father, and the dogs Fındık and Fiştik. It is another still to think of all those who welcomed, who never had the time to introduce themselves: the woman at Sakarya who threw a packet of biscuits my way as she boarded a dolmuş; the villagers in Uludere who ran over to us to hand over some freshly baked bread; and the farmer in Hisarcık who wandered over to our camp to offer our group some fresh tomatoes.

Occasionally, such a tangible difference in culture led me to ponder the experience more deeply. I was reminded occasionally that I might not have received the same welcome had I been a lone female, or another ethnicity. My reception might have changed quite dramatically had I been walking in a different direction, away from a war zone, towards a place of refuge. However, as much as I was aware that such generosity might not be applied equally to all, I also had ample time to consider how different such an ethos was to English societal norms. I was intermittently reminded that it was orders of magnitude easier for a Briton to visit Turkey than the other way around, and that a Turkish man walking across England by himself might not receive the same welcome as I had done. Ultimately, I will never know. Although I was left questioning whether my own nation would match the same level of warmth, or more pertinently whether I would, such scenarios remain hypothetical. All one can do is reflect and learn, and try to do right.

On the topic of ethical considerations, one lesson taught repeatedly from Day one onwards was just how hard it could be to balance my needs and desire to meet people, with respect for the privacy and livelihoods of those I now lived alongside. Being such a subjective question in the first instance, before adding in the complications of culture, gender, language and age gaps, getting the balance right between interacting with people and avoiding imposing myself was an extremely difficult line to tread. For instance, I made it an unofficial rule to avoid ever approaching people's houses to ask for things directly, unless absolutely desperate. I would accept hospitality if offered, but refused to do anything that might resemble begging. It was likely an over-stringent standard to hold myself to, and I am sure many more homes would have welcomed me with open arms had I knocked on more doors. Whilst I maintain that this was a good ethical standard to maintain, taking the initiative and engaging more proactively could have created more opportunities. Yet, even when erring on the side of caution as I did, the willingness of ordinary people to offer whatever they could is a testament to that tangible culture of welcome that, I hope, I have done some service to by writing about.

More broadly, the inherently hybrid nature of the trip was as challenging as it was rewarding. There were always compromises to be made between immersion in culture and completion of the journey. Oscillating between 'walking brain' and 'cultural brain' continuously took a particular mental toll during the first fortnight on the road. One was not 'rest' from the other, as much as a different form of exertion. Both could be exhausting. Asking myself *'when do I need to set off by?', 'have I got everything?', 'where will I get food/water/shelter?',* before switching into the complexities of interacting in a new, challenging environment, meant that time on the road rarely included time to fully relax. Although doing so became easier as the journey progressed, I felt the physical side progressively eclipsed the cultural aspects of the expedition, which I would have preferred to avoid.

However, as much as the twin challenges clashed with one another, I remain convinced that seeing the country entirely by foot unlocked it in two unique ways. Whilst physically walking every single metre between Kefken and Konyaaltı came with undeniably unpleasant segments, they only amplified the unspoiled, the untrodden, and the utterly beautiful when they arrived. It was an immense privilege to visit some truly pristine places. The endless highways, rubbish-encrusted embankments, and sprawling masses of abandoned concrete that lay between them, was the price to pay for such scenes. Paying for them in discomfort, deposited in drips of sweat, made those places all the more meaningful to stumble upon.

In reflection, walking the route in its totality has also given me a strange sense of retrospective completeness. Although only familiar with that thin, long strip of land adjacent to my route, there was nothing along that 620-

kilometre corridor that I did not experience. Knowing so, in an obscure, indescribable way, has made the whole experience last more enduringly in memory. It has given my recollections an unusual longevity and reality. That comprehensive sense of completion would have felt undeniably different, I am convinced, had I either taken another mode of transport, or hopped around. Even if I can't recall every step that I took, I once could. Walking cuts no corners.

As already expressed, nothing immediately transformative happened when I reached the sea. Yet, whilst writing this recollection, fourteen months of life has since revealed more subtle ways in which the experience was profoundly changing. Getting used to walking in bounds of days seemed to, after a while, make the world seem smaller, whilst remaining intimate. Previously used to walking for a few days at a time in Britain's national parks, the horizon was somewhere far away, difficult to hit. Having reached it, a warm vehicle, a cleansing shower, and a hot fire would await. Somehow in my mind, those aspects needed to await the end of the trail, to make the trip achievable. Adjusting to that absence transformed that perspective. Knowing firstly the only way out was onwards, and secondly that doing so was achievable, has somehow permanently brought the horizon a little closer.

The world has shrunk since Turkey. It is quite possible, as a human being, to fly over hills, forests, rivers, quarries, piles of dumped rubbish, and packs of feral dogs. It takes only three elements: the ability to let one's mind wander as one's legs work; the ability to communicate the bare essentials of life to the kindest, warmest, and most trusting people one will ever encounter; and the ability to live in the dirt by the road for a few days.

Timothy David Chattell was born in Cheltenham, England. He was educated at Peter Symonds College, Winchester, before attending the University of Nottingham as an undergraduate, and the London School of Economics as a postgraduate scholar. When not travelling, he lives in Hampshire with his family and their Collie-Spaniel, Tess.

Printed in Great Britain
by Amazon